AF600152

VOCATION TO THE PRIESTHOOD: ITS CANONICAL CONCEPT

THE CATHOLIC UNIVERSITY OF AMERICA
CANON LAW STUDIES
No. 293

Vocation to the Priesthood: Its Canonical Concept

A HISTORICAL SYNOPSIS AND A COMMENTARY

BY

AIDAN CARR, O.F.M.Conv., S.T.D., J.C.L., LL.B.
Priest of the Province of the Immaculate Conception
St. Anthony-on-Hudson, Rensselaer, New York

A DISSERTATION
SUBMITTED TO THE FACULTY OF THE SCHOOL OF CANON LAW
OF THE CATHOLIC UNIVERSITY OF AMERICA IN PARTIAL
FULFILLMENT OF THE REQUIREMENTS FOR THE
DEGREE OF DOCTOR OF CANON LAW

THE CATHOLIC UNIVERSITY OF AMERICA PRESS
WASHINGTON, D.C.
1950

Revisores ex parte Ordinis:

Eduardus Roelker, S.T.D., J.C.D.
Gulielmus D'Arcy, O.F.M.Conv., S.T.L., Ph. D.

Imprimi Potest:

Franciscus Edic, O.F.M.Conv.,
Minister Provincialis.

Syracusis in N.E., die 6 julii 1949.

Nihil Obstat:

Ferdinandus Mayer, O.F.M.Conv., S.T.M., J.C.D.
Censor Librorum

Albani, die 4 novembris 1949.

Imprimatur:

✠ Edmundus F. Gibbons, D.D.,
Episcopus Albanensis in N.E.

Albani, die 8 novembris 1949.

The Abbey Press, St. Meinrad, Ind.

TABLE OF CONTENTS

FOREWORD

The purpose of this dissertation is to examine the juridical signification of vocation to the priesthood. The problem of the precise nature, elements and effects of that vocation by which some men are chosen by God and by His Church to devote themselves exclusively to the sacred ministry is assuredly one of profound interest and importance to all who are concerned with the extension of God's Kingdom on earth: a sublime work that depends in a most special way upon an unfailing supply of worthy priests.

The phrase "vocation to the priesthood" is itself somewhat nebulous in character, and this seemingly intangible quality has sometimes—quite understandably—caused some who are otherwise interested in the subject of the priestly call to shy clear of a sustained study of it. Still others have found in this apparent elusiveness of the vocational concept the occasion for treating the problem with an unwarranted air of pietism, the while neglecting to set forth necessary canonical (and dogmatic) precisions.

Accordingly a scientific juridical-theological approach to the question of vocation indeed seems justified, particularly in view of recent pontifical acts emphasizing the necessity for an exact appraisal and appreciation of the concept of vocation to the priesthood. This need was strikingly indicated in the opening words of the Instruction of the Sacred Congregation of the Sacraments, *Quam ingens,* issued on December 27, 1930:

> How great is the harm done to the Church and to the salvation of souls by those who, without having a vocation from God, presume to undertake the priestly ministry, a responsibility which would be a serious one even for angels, no one surely will question. Hence, those who have been placed by the Holy Ghost must, in order to guard the Church and the faithful from many great wrongs, use the greatest care that access to so great an office be

> denied those to whom, for want of a priestly vocation, the words of Our Lord are applicable: "Amen, amen, I say to you: he that entereth not by the door into the sheepfold, but climbeth up another way, the same is a thief and a robber" (John, X, 1).[1]

The consideration of a certain compenetration of theological and legal notions has proved inescapable in the present work, but the writer has consistently sought to employ the conclusions of theology only in that measure in which they serve to illuminate juridical principles. The concomitance of these two elements has indeed proved so invariable that to divorce legislation from doctrine would be to destroy the perspective required for a clear grasp of the salient aspects of the vocational problem.

This study proposes to be at once speculative and practical. It is speculative in so far as it analyzes and relates cognate theories of law and theology. It is practical in so far as from these theories, as they have been expressed in concrete legislation, norms have been derived as an aid for those who are obliged by ecclesiastical law to determine the probable presence of an all important vocation in candidates for Orders. It is intended also as a guide for those whose ministry as confessor or spiritual director frequently brings them face to face with the vital question, "Has this youth a probable vocation to the priesthood?"

The method of investigation determined upon is to examine the constituent parts both of divine and of ecclesiastical vocation, and by synthetically relating those parts thus to achieve a unified concept of the priestly vocation. It will be observed that the historical synopsis and the canonical commentary have been integrated. It is believed that this type of presentation lends itself more readily to a lucid and orderly treatment of the subject of this particular study.

The writer takes this opportunity to express his profound sense of gratitude to his religious superiors for the granted

[1] § 1, n. 1—*Acta Apostolicae Sedis* (Romae, 1909—), XXIII (1934), 120 (hereafter cited *AAS*). (English text in Bouscaren, *The Canon Law Digest* 2 vols., Milwaukee: Bruce, 1934-1943, p. 463.)

permission for advanced studies in Canon Law, to the Faculty of the School of Canon Law of the Catholic University of America for their helpful direction and constructive criticism in the projected work, and to all those without whose encouragement this study would not have been realized, particularly the Rev. Edgar Holden, O.F.M.Conv., S.T.D., to whom it is dedicated.

PART I

THE DIVINE VOCATION TO THE PRIESTHOOD

CHAPTER I

THE NATURE OF THE PRIESTLY OFFICE

The Catholic priesthood instituted by Christ[1] was prefigured in the Old Law,[2] but the Christian priesthood far excels its prototype, because it is able to remit sin and is destined to be of eternal duration.[3] The priesthood is essentially an office constituting its incumbents mediators between God and men, "for every high priest taken from among men is appointed for men in the things pertaining to God. . . ."[4] And Christ's Church which is served by that

[1] Cf. John, XV, 16; Luke, V, 19; Conc. Trident., sess. XXIII, *de ordine*, can. 3: "Si quis dixerit, ordinem sive sacram ordinationem non esse vere et proprie sacramentum a Christo Domino institutum . . . a.s."—Mansi, *Sacrorum Conciliorum Nova et Amplissima Collectio* (53 vols. in 60, Paris, Leipzig, Arnhem, 1901-1927), XXXIII, 140 (hereafter cited Mansi).

[2] Ex., XXVIII, 1; Eccles., XLV, 19. Cf. St. Thomas Aquinas, *Summa Theologica* (6 vols., Taurinorum Augustae: Marietti, 1938), IIIa, q. 22, a. 1 ad 2 um: ". . . sacerdotium veteris legis erat figura sacerdotii Christi . . . ."; Conc. Trident., sess. XXIII, *de ordine*, c. 1: ". . . in ea [Ecclesia catholica] novum esse visibile et externum sacerdotium, in quod vetus translatum est."—Mansi, XXXIII, 138; Pius XI, ep. encycl. *Ad catholici sacerdotii fastigium*, 20 dec. 1935: "Atqui Veteris Testamenti sacerdotium maiestatem gloriamque suam non aliunde sumebat, nisi quod illud praenuntiabat novi aeternique Testamenti a Iesu Christo datum, veri scilicet Dei verique hominis sanguine constitutum."—*AAS*, XXVIII (1936), 10.

[3] St. Thomas Aquinas, *Summa Theologica*, IIIa, q. 22, a. 6.

[4] Heb., V, 1. Cf. St. Thomas Aquinas, *Summa Theologica*, IIIa, q. 22, a. 1: ". . . proprie officium sacerdotis est esse mediatorem inter Deum et populum."; Pius XI, ep. encycl. *Ad catholici sacerdotii fastigium, 20 dec.* 1935: "Nullo non tempore genus humanum sacerdotum necessitatem expertum est, virorum scilicet, qui, ex officio legitime concredito, Dei hominumque conciliatores essent . . . ."—*AAS*, XXVIII (1936), 8.

priesthood, is a divine-human society with a sacred hierarchy distinct from the laity, and having for its formal object the spiritual welfare of all men. The divinely providential means for the accomplishment of that object include the priests—men set apart from the body of the faithful by ordination,[5] a sacred rite conferring upon its recipients spiritual powers peculiar to the sacrament of Orders.[6]

Christ's selection of His first priests is described in Holy Scripture as a vocation: *"Vocavit ad se, quos voluit ipse."*[7] This calling was an invitation to share in Christ's own priesthood, and the subsequent ordination and mission made the priest truly an *alter Christus.* By his sacerdotal character the priest not only represents Christ but is identified with Him in the performance of sacred functions. Thus there exists between Christ and His priest not only a succession and a continuity, but an identity of ministry in so far as the priest participates immediately in Christ's priesthood.[8] So intimate is this share in the priesthood of Christ that St. Thomas Aquinas (1225-1274) declared that a priest, as priest, acts in the Person of Christ, Who is the *"fons totius sacerdotii."*[9]

[5] Canons 107; 948. Cf. Conc. Trident., sess. XXIII, *de ordine,* c. 4—Mansi, XXXIII, 139.

[6] Cf. canon 109; Matt., IV, 19; Luke, VIII, 10; St. Thomas Aquinas, *Summa Theologica,* IIIa, q. 84, a. 4: "... in sacramento ordinis, in quo confertur quaedam excellentia potestatis in divinis mysteriis ...."

[7] Mark, III, 13.

[8] Cf. Thomassinus, *Vetus et Nova Ecclesiae Disciplina* (10 vols., Magontiaci, 1787), Pars II, lib. II, cap. I, n. 3 (hereafter cited Thomassinus): "... participatio quaedam fit et imago expressissima authoritatis, qua in filium incarnatum pollet Deus et Pater, et qua illum [Christum] in pontificem gignit: 'Ego hodie genui te.' "; Cappello, *Summa Iuris Publici Ecclesiastici* (5. ed., Romae: Typis Pontificiae Universitatis Gregorianae, 1943), n. 367.

[9] *Summa Theologica,* IIIa, q. 22, a. 4. Cf. Pius XI, ep. encycl. *Ad catholici sacerdotii fastigium,* 20 dec. 1935: "Minister Christi sacerdos: divini igitur Redemptoris quasi instrumentum est .... Quin immo ipse, quod iure meritoque dicere sollemne habemus, 'alter est Christus', cum eius gerat personam secundum illud: 'sicut misit me Pater, et ego mitto vos' ...."—*AAS,* XXVIII (1936), 10.

The constitution of the Apostles as the first bishops conferred upon them a threefold power: 1) *ministerium;* 2) *magisterium;* 3) *regimen;* powers necessary for the perpetuity of the Church inasmuch as their exercise guarantees an unceasing administration of the sacraments and the continuance of the Christian cult through the *ministerium;* the preservation of revealed truth through the *magisterium;* and the enactment of law and its sanction through the *regimen.*[10] By divine institution only bishops possess this triple power fully[11] and so are superior to simple priests,[12] who are ordained for the offering of the sacrifice of the Mass and the administration of the sacraments other than Orders and Confirmation.[13]

While the sacerdotal character is had in both bishops and simple priests, yet it exists more completely in the former,[14] while both possess the essential note of the *ministerium:* the capacity to consecrate the Eucharist and to remit sin.[15] The sacrificial and sacramental functions of the priesthood pertain to the *ministerium,* which in turn is related to the *regimen*—the social authority of the Church—only in the

[10] Cf. Cappello, *Summa Iuris Publici Ecclesiastici,* n. 141.

[11] Cf. canons 329, §§ 1, 2; 335, § 1.

[12] Cf. Conc. Trident., sess. XXIII, *de ordine,* can. 7: "Si quis dixerit, episcopos non esse presbyteris superiores . . . a.s."—Mansi, XXXIII, 140.

[13] Cf. canons 802; 951; 782, §1; Conc. Trident., sess. XXIII, *de ordine,* cans. 1, 7.—Mansi, XXXIII, 139-140.

[14] Cf. Thomassinus, Pars I, lib. I, cap. I, n. 3: "Episcopatus a Christo instituendus, plenissima erat sacerdotalis dignitatis et potestatis ubertas . . . ."; Conc. Trident., sess. XXIII, *de ordine,* c. 4: ". . . si quis . . . omnes pari inter se potestate spirituali praeditos affirmet, nihil aliud facere videtur quam ecclesiasticam hierarchiam . . . confundere . . . ."—Mansi, XXXIII, 139.

[15] Cf. Conc. Trident., sess. XXIII, *de ordine,* c. 1: "Sacrificium et sacerdotium ita Dei ordinatione coniuncta sunt . . . in novo testamento sanctum Eucharistiae sacrificium visibile ex Domini institutione catholica Ecclesia acceperit . . . . Hoc autem ab eodem Domino Salvatore nostro institutum esse . . . in sacerdotio potestatem traditam consecrandi, offerendi et ministrandi corpus et sanguinem eius, nec non et peccata dimittendi et retinendi . . . ."—Mansi, XXXIII, 138.

measure that the actual exercise of the ministry is governed by norms set up by the ecclesiastical society itself. The power of Holy Orders, which are constitutive of the *ministerium,* flows from ordination, while the *regimen* (and the *magisterium*) depends upon a canonical mission.[16] It is in relation to the *sacerdotium*[17] precisely as it implies the *ministerium* that divine vocation must be considered, for only the power annexed to the *ministerium* is proper to both the episcopacy and to the simple priesthood.

[16] Cf. Wernz (1842-1914)-Vidal (1868-1939), *Ius Canonicum* (7 vols. in 8, Romae: Apud Aedes Universitatis Gregorianae, 1923-1938), II, n. 48.

[17] The word "*sacerdotium*" is a generic one, including two species: the episcopacy (*sacerdotium primi ordinis*) and the simple priesthood (*sacerdotium secundi ordinis.*).—Cf. *dictum Gratiani* ad c. 1, D. XXI. Often the canonical sources employ the generic term, a practice that appeared as early as the Council of Laodicea (343/381), which used *ἱερατεῖον* in a canon on the episcopacy.—Bruns, *Canones Apostolorum et Conciliorum saec. IV, V, VI, VII* (2 vols., Berolini, 1839), I, 74 (hereafter cited Bruns), and as recently as the Council of Trent (1545-1563): sess. XXIII, *de ordine,* c. 1—Mansi, XXXIII, 139. The English equivalent of the Greek *ἱερατεῖον* is "a sanctuary"; "clergy".—H.G. Liddell, *Greek-English Lexicon* (8. ed., New York, 1897), p. 695.

CHAPTER II

THE CONSTITUENTS OF THE DIVINE VOCATION

ARTICLE 1. THE SOURCE OF THE DIVINE VOCATION

Whenever in the Old Testament there was question of God's special concerns, particularly with regard to the divine economy for man's salvation, God explicitly and unequivocally called certain persons to the task of co-operating with Him in the accomplishment of His designs. In no instance is this more evident than in the call to the priesthood addressed to Aaron and his posterity by Yahweh: "Take unto thee also Aaron thy brother with his sons, from among the children of Israel, that they may minister to me in the priest's office. . . ."[1]

That this sacerdotal office was restricted to those who were divinely called is apparent from the warning to any "stranger" who might presumptuously attempt to enter upon the ministry of the altar: "But thou shalt appoint Aaron and his sons over the service of priesthood. The stranger that approacheth to minister, shall be put to death."[2] This divine institution and protection of the Jewish priesthood was consistently acknowledged by Hebrew leaders and was strictly observed by them.[3]

The Christian priesthood is the continuation and perfection of the Jewish priesthood,[4] and just as did the latter, it also depends upon God's Providence for its origin and perpetuation. Since there is no lawful power that is not ultimately from God, so there can be no lawful agent of that

[1] Ex., XXVIII, 1.

[2] Num., III, 10. Cf. Eccles., XLV, 23. Cf. Franciscus de Hummelauer (1530-1596), *Commentarius in Numeros* (Paris, 1899), p. 30: "Quem-*externum* interpretatur Sa 'non aaronitam', ut igitur moneantur levitae, ne sibi sacerdotium arrogare attentent . . . ."

[3] Cf. Num., XVI, 5; II Par., XXVI, 17-18.

[4] Cf. St. Thomas Aquinas, *Summa Theologica*, IIIa, q. 22, a. 4.

power other than one called by Him to the exercise of it.[5] The minister of the cult of a natural or man-made religion might well be designated simply by the will of the people whom he represented,[6] but in the supernatural religion which is divinely revealed it must be otherwise. For when God discloses the form of worship by which He wishes to be honored, He confides its ministry to whom He pleases, and whosoever dares to intrude himself upon that ministry without some favorable manifestation of the divine will is therefore a usurper.[7]

Even Christ, the first and only High Priest of the New Dispensation, did not assume the priesthood without a call from the Father by Whom that priesthood was willed. It was the Father's eternal decree that Christ be anointed with the priestly dignity in a pre-eminent manner and indeed from the very inception of His earthly life:

> And no man takes the honor to himself; he takes it who is called by God, as Aaron was. So also Christ did not glorify himself with the high priesthood, but he who spoke to him, "Thou art my son, I this day have begotten thee."[8]

In a commentary on this text St. Thomas Aquinas recognized the operation of God's will both in the institution of the Christian priesthood and in the vocation to that office when he taught that it is inordinate for one to seek by his own powers that which simply exceeds his natural capacity.[9]

The invitation extended to the first priests of the New Law was delivered in a manner that showed clearly its di-

[5] Cf. Rom., XIII, 1.

[6] Cf. St. Thomas Aquinas, *Summa Theologica,* Ia-IIae, q. 103, a. 1 ad 3um.

[7] Cf. Prat, *La Theologie de Saint Paul* (Paris, 1908), I, 529. "Called" (*vocatus-κλητός*) in the New Testament has always the sense of "called by God."—*Ibid.,* 344.

[8] Heb., V, 4-6.

[9] *Commentaria in Omnes S. Pauli Apostoli Epistolas-Ad Hebraeos* (2 vols., Romae: Marietti, 1917), II, 344: "Hoc est enim contra naturam, quod aliquid perducat se ad statum altiorem sua natura...."

vine origin,[10] and moreover that both the priesthood and its vocation have God for their source was further strikingly emphasized in connection with the initial call to the Catholic priesthood: "You have not chosen me, but I have chosen you, and have appointed you that you should go and bear fruit, and that your fruit should remain. . . ."[11]

The manner in which the Apostles invoked heavenly guidance in the choice of a successor to Judas[12] attested their consciousness that the sacred ministry's origin and continued renewal actually rested upon positive divine decree. The words of Christ, "Amen, amen, I say to you, he who enters not by the door into the sheepfold, but climbs up another way, is a thief and a robber. But he who enters by the door is shepherd of the sheep. . . . Amen, amen, I say to you, I am the door of the sheep,"[13] are interpreted by exegetes as an example of divine causality in the matter of vocation to the sacerdotal dignity.[14]

ARTICLE 2. The Nature of the Divine Vocation

Cardinal Gasparri (1852-1934) provided canonists with a descriptive definition of divine vocation when he stated that everyone—save those who impugn Providence and the

[10] Mark, III, 13.

[11] John, XV, 16. Cf. Knabenbauer, *Commentarius in Evangelium secundum Ioannem* (Paris, 1904), p. 466: ". . . ipse [Christus] enim prior eos dilexit et ad dignitatem praeclaram eos elegit . . . in discipulos et apostolos; ego vos ad meam sequelam vocavi invitatione externa et gratia interna; in apostolos elegit ex discipulis quos voluit ipse."

[12] Acts, I, 24-25.

[13] John, X, 1-3, 9.

[14] Cf. Lagrange, *Evangile selon Saint Marc* (Paris, 1911), p. 58: "L'élection vient de Jésus; leur part est de le rejoindre . . . ."; Knabenbauer, *Commentarius in Evangelium secundum Ioannem*, p. 338: "Cum Jesus (in Jo., X, 7) dicat se esse ostium, illi designantur qui non vocati ab eo sibi munus docendi et regendi arrogant, vel generatim qui sine vocatione divina eiusmodi dignitatem usurpant . . . ."; St. Thomas Aquinas, *Commentaria in Omnes S. Pauli Apostoli Epistolas—II Tim.*, II, 231: "Origo Apostolatus est voluntas Dei."

supernatural order—admits that God chooses certain individuals for the priesthood independently of their merits, and endows them with such qualities as are requisite for the proper performance of the priestly duties.[15] Many (†1922) used the same description, but laid particular stress upon the element of divine destination of determined persons to the priesthood.[16]

The delineation of divine vocation offered by these authors may conveniently be divided into two constituent parts:

1. A divine decree selecting certain men for the priesthood independently of their personal merit.
2. Consequent upon this operation of Providence, those chosen by that decree to become priests are endowed with such gifts as render them apt for the sacred ministry.

The implications of these two elements are now to be examined.

A. THE DIVINE DECREE OF VOCATION

In the Old Testament the dignity and power of the legal priesthood were perpetuated through the blood-line of Aaron, whose sons became priests simply by the accident of birth into the priestly caste,[17] while in the New Dispensation

[15] *Tractatus Canonicus de Sacra Ordinatione* (2 vols., Parisiis, 1893), n. 110 (hereafter cited *De Sacra Ordinatione*): "Omnes admittunt, si excipias illos qui divinam providentiam aut ordinem supernaturalem detrectant, Deum, independenter a creaturae meritis, aliquos prae aliis eligere ad statum sacerdotalem ... eosdemque praeparare dotibus seu corporis seu animi congruis ad sacra ministeria digne et laudabiliter obeunda. Hic divinae supernaturalis providentiae actus est divina vocatio ad statum clericalem."

[16] *Praelectiones de Sacra Ordinatione* (Parisiis, 1905), p. 204: "Quo Deus aliquem *destinat* ad statum clericalem. En *actus ipse vocationis*, nempe *destinatio* alicujus in individuo ad hunc statum, et idcirco ejus electio prae mille aliis." (Italics are Many's.) Cf. Cappello, *Tractatus Canonico-Moralis de Sacramentis* (3 vols. in 6, Vol. II, Pars III [*De Sacra Ordinatione*], Romae: Marietti, 1935), Vol. II, Pars III, n. 366.

[17] Num., III, 3: "These [are] the names of the sons of Aaron the priests that were anointed, and whose hands were filled and consecrated, to do the functions of priesthood."

the Christian priesthood is intended to be shared by men of whatever race, provided only that they are divinely called.[18] This call for which every Christian man is potentially or remotely eligible is in fact given to but a few[19] who are providentially selected for reasons ultimately hidden in the inscrutable intellect and will of God,[20] and these reasons transcend the ambit, not merely of canonical inquiry, but of human understanding.

The divine decree by which one is singled out for the sacred priesthood may be considered under a twofold aspect: 1) as the act of selecting exists in God Himself; 2) as that act produces a result in the one called.[21] If the decree is viewed under the first aspect, there is realized vocation in its active modality: God inviting someone, by an operation of grace upon the soul, to desire and to seek the priesthood. Pope Pius XI (1922-1939) referred to this in his encyclical *"Ad catholici sacerdotii fastigium"* of December 20, 1935.[22] If the decree is viewed under the second aspect, there is realized vocation in its passive acceptation: the entity of

[18] Cf. Gasparri, *De Sacra Ordinatione*, n. 109: "In veteri lege Deus sacerdotium reservaverat Aaron ejusque filiis ... Christus D. nihil hujusmodi in nova lege constituit ... Deus ad statum clericalem appellat quos vult, ex omni tribu et lingua et populo et natione ...."

[19] Cf. the observation of Pope Zosimus (417-418) relevant to the priestly dignity: "Rarum est enim omne quod magnum est."—C.2, D. LIX; Jaffé, *Regesta Pontificum Romanorum ab condita Ecclesia ad annum post Christum natum MCXCVIII* (2. ed. correctam et auctam auspiciis Gulielmi Wattenbach curaverunt S. Loewenfeld, F. Kaltenbrunner, P. Ewald, 2 vols. in 1, Lipsiae, 1885-1888), n. 339 (hereafter cited Jaffé).

[20] Cf. St. Thomas Aquinas, *Summa Theologica*, Ia-IIae, q. 13, a. 2: "... electio sit praeacceptio unius respectu alterius ...."; Pius XI, ep. encycl. *Ad catholici sacerdotii fastigium*, 20 dec. 1935: "... divinitus facta selectio ...."—*AAS*, XXVIII (1936), 48.

[21] Many, *Praelectiones de Sacra Ordinatione*, p. 204.

[22] *AAS*, XXVIII (1936), 23, 40. Cf. Pius XII, ep. ap., *Haud mediocrem*, 22 nov. 1941: "... quam quidem vocationem praecipuum supernae gratiae supernique amoris signum agnoscent, itemque sibi suisque omnibus caelestium munerum fontem."—*AAS*, XXXIV (1942), 237.

grace manifested by the presence in the one called of such qualities as comprise aptitude for the lawful reception of Orders. "Vocation", as used in the present study, is ordinarily and more properly understood in the second sense: the execution, in time, of the divine plan.

This distinction between active and passive vocation to the priesthood is predicated upon an analogous teaching of St. Thomas Aquinas relative to the vocation to glory. The two vocations possess a true affinity inasmuch as both are parts of Providence.[23] In this connection the Angelic Doctor taught:

> It must be said that predestination is a certain part of Providence.... But the execution of Providence, which is called governing, is indeed passively in the things governed, but is active in the thing governing.... But vocation is the execution of predestination.[24]

Thus the divine decree of vocation to Orders considered either actively or passively is a special act of Providence in the sense that God makes specific provision that His indefectible Church shall never want for worthy ministers,[25] and to the fulfillment of this end destines only those whom He has eternally elected and equipped for the lofty and exacting demands of the Catholic priesthood.[26]

[23] Cf. Many, *Praelectiones de Sacra Ordinatione*, p. 204.

[24] *Summa Theologica*, Ia, q. 23, a. 2: "Dictum est enim quod praedestinatio est quaedam pars providentiae.... Sed executio providentiae, quae gubernatio dicitur, passive quidem est in gubernatis, active autem est in gubernante.... Est autem executio praedestinationis vocatio...."

[25] Cf. *Summa Theologica*, Suppl., q. 36, a. 4 ad 1um: "Deus numquam ita deserit Ecclesiam suam, quin inveniantur idonei ministri sufficientes ad necessitatem plebis, si digni promoverentur, et indigni repellerentur."

[26] Cf. Tanquerey, *Synopsis Theologiae Moralis et Pastoralis* (3 vols., ed. 5., New York: Benziger, 1907-1908), Vol. I, n. 1157: "Cum enim Deus sit sapiens et providus, quos eligit ad sublimia et ardua sacerdotii munera, iis ab aeterno paravit omnes dotes ad haec munera digne ac laudabiliter obeunda necessarias...."; Hurtaud, *La Vocation au Sacerdoce* (2. ed., Paris, 1911), p. 58.

An awareness of the primacy of grace in the conferring of each vocation prompted Pope Pius XI to describe vocation as a divine inspiration sowed in the generous hearts of young men, there to be cultivated and protected by those entrusted with the aspirant's ecclesiastical formation.[27] And the intent of the law of the Code is similarly manifest when priests, especially pastors, are urged to nurture in likely youths the "seed of divine vocation."[28] Led on by the grace of vocation placed in the soul consequent upon a special predilection of supernatural Providence, the recipient of the vocational grace desires the priesthood as a concrete good, a state which, while primarily contributing to the welfare of others, can nevertheless be conducive to his own sanctification.

1. *The Function of Grace*

If the Thomistic doctrine is invoked to explain the nature and activity of the efficacious vocational grace—one which actually results in the subject's ordination—it must be concluded that the eternal decree takes effect in time through physical premotion. Under this influence the hitherto undetermined will is in fact determined by the *gratia operans* to elicit the choice of the priesthood. The motion of the grace is intrinsically efficacious and precedes, in the order of causality, the will's free election. Inasmuch as this predetermination is physical and not simply a moral one, it does not merely persuade or induce the subject to act, but rather leads the will freely although infallibly from the potentiality of willing the priesthood to the actuality of willing it. Since an efficacious grace of vocation is in reality a series of graces, such additional steps are undertaken by the subject (now himself acting under the *gratia cooperans*)

[27] Cf. ep. encycl. *Ad catholici sacerdotii fastigium,* 20 dec. 1935, n. III: "Nihilominus nullae ex homini permissis industriis curisque neglegendae sunt, quae illuc in primis spectent, ut in generosis iuvenum animis divinitus acceptus afflatus quam diligentissime excitetur. . . ."—*AAS,* XXVIII (1936), 45.

[28] Canon 1353: ". . . divinaeque in eis vocationis germen foveant."

and external conditions so come to pass, that ordination is in fact attained.[29]

In a broad sense it can be said that a vocation may be "lost", either culpably[30] or inculpably.[31] When it appears that a vocation has been lost either through one's own fault or otherwise,[32] we may conclude that the one who "lost" the vocation may have been divinely *prepared* for the priesthood (by his suitability for it) but not divinely *elected* to it. If the Thomistic doctrine relative to the intrinsic efficacy of grace be invoked, it is evident that a truly efficacious series of graces was simply not present, for while the liberty of the human will to resist grace remains unimpaired even under efficacious grace,[33] nevertheless such a grace is not in fact resisted, and so without exception the grace accomplishes the end for which it has been given. The will of the called individual assents to the vocational grace[34] and ex-

[29] Cf. Hervé, *Manuale Theologiae Dogmaticae* (4 vols., Vol. III, 18. ed. Westminster, Md.: Newman, 1943), Vol. III, n. 115; Garrigou-Lagrange, *De Gratia* (Roma: Marietti, 1946), pp. 140-141; 205-206.

[30] Cf. S. C. de Sacramentis, instr. *Quam ingens*, § 3, n. 2: "Si vero res eo deducatur, ut clare pateat subdiaconum ad diaconatum promovendum, vel vocationem reapse numquam habuisse, aut eamdem corruptis moribus amisisse, tunc res erit intimius perscrutanda. . . ." —*AAS*, XXIII (1931), 125.

[31] Cf. St. Thomas Aquinas, *Summa Theologica*, IIa-IIae, q. 189, a. 10: "Nec propter hoc ostenditur non esse ex Deo quod aliqui retrocedunt: non enim omne quod a Deo est, incorruptibile est. . . ."

[32] Cf. Gasparri, *De Sacra Ordinatione*, n. 110: "Haec autem divina vocatio ecclesiastica esse non solet absoluta, et auferre humanam libertatem, hinc frustrari potest sive ex culpa tum ipsius personae vocatae tum aliorum, sive extra culpam."

[33] Cf. St. Thomas Aquinas, *Summa Theologica*, Ia-IIae, q. 10, a. 4: "Quia igitur voluntas est activum principium non determinatum ad unum, sed indifferenter se habens ad multa; sic Deus ipsam movet, quod non ex necessitate ad unum determinat, sed remanet motus eius contingens, et non necessarius, nisi in his ad quae naturaliter movetur."

[34] Cf. Garrigou-Lagrange, *De Gratia*, p. 209: "Concilium (Trident.) non dicit (in sess. VI, *de justificatione*, can. 4) quod homo dissentit quandoque de facto, sed dicit: '*potest* dissentire, si velit', scil. *remanet potentia ad oppositum*, sed sub gratia efficaci homo numquam vult resistere, nec resistit, alioquin gratia non esset efficax seu, esset con-

ternal conditions are so disposed by Providence that the course of the individual towards final ordination is in no wise effectively impeded.[35]

If the priesthood be considered under its primary and usual aspect as a means to sanctify others rather than to sanctify the one possessing the sacerdotal character,[36] it is evident that its social purpose imparts to the priestly office a certain affinity to a *gratia gratis data,* i.e., a charismatic quality.[37] But more precisely according to the common Thomistic teaching, the priesthood is a grace of *ministratio* and *operatio.*[38] In so far as the priesthood partakes of the nature of a *gratia gratis data,* strictly considered its vocation cannot be merited,[39] but if the secondary aspect of the priesthood be considered, namely the sanctification of oneself through the exercise of the priestly functions, then it must be held that the grace of vocation can, in a broader sense, be the object of merit in the measure that a vocation

---

tradictio in terminis; scil. alioquin gratia non faceret ut faciamus." (Italics are Garrigou-Lagrange's.)

[35] Cf. St. Thomas Aquinas, *Summa Theologica,* Ia. q. 23, a. 6: "Sed non omnia quae providentiae subduntur, necessaria sunt; sed quaedam contingenter eveniunt, secundum conditionem causarum proximarum, quas ad tales effectus divina providentia ordinavit...."

[36] *Ibid.,* Suppl., q. 35, a. 1 ad 1um: "Ordo datur non in remedium unius personae, sed totius Ecclesiae."

[37] *Ibid.,* Ia-IIae, q. 111, a. 1: "Alia gratia vero per quam unus homo cooperatur alteri ad hoc quod ad Deum reducatur; huiusmodi autem donum vocatur *gratia gratis data*...." It seems from St. Thomas' answer to an objection in the *Summa Theologica,* Suppl., q. 35, a. 1 ad 2um, that he taught that the priesthood is a *gratia gratis data.* According to Garrigou-Lagrange, *De Gratia,* p. 125, Suarez placed the sacerdotal character among the charismatic graces.

[38] Cf. Garrigou-Lagrange, *op. cit.,* p. 127: "...ministratio vero seu ministerium dicit auctoritatem exercendi aliquem actum in ordine ad alios homines, ut apostolatus, episcopatus, presbiteratus, et quaecumque praelatio."

[39] Gasparri, *De Sacra Ordinatione,* n. 110: "...Deum, independenter a creaturae meritis, aliquos prae aliis eligere ad statum sacerdotalem...." Cf. Garrigou-Lagrange, *op. cit.,* p. 123.

to it may indeed lead to the performance of many salutary acts in the sacred ministry.[40]

B. THE CONSEQUENCE OF THE DIVINE DECREE OF VOCATION

Providence as a part of divine prudence[41] orders things to a determined end through proportionate means. In relation to the priestly vocation this order takes effect in granting to the one called such qualities as fit him for the priesthood, for if God selects someone for the clerical state, He will, in His infinite wisdom and power, prepare for the subject of the vocational grace such talents of soul and body as are requisite for the attainment of the priesthood and the worthy discharge of its annexed obligations.[42]

This conclusion is deducible from the apposite principle formulated by St. Thomas Aquinas that states that those whom God elects for some duty are so divinely prepared and disposed that they are, by that very election, rendered suited to the task before them.[43] And this general principle is specifically applied by the Angelic Doctor in the case of the priesthood.[44] Thus the grace by which one is made

[40] Cf. *Summa Theologica,* Ia-IIae, q. 114, a. 10: "... omnia illa quae ordinantur ut ducentia ad hunc [ultimum] finem; et talia simpliciter cadunt sub merito." It is not in itself a sin for one to refuse what he believes may be a vocation to the priesthood since this is an office in no wise required for salvation. This refusal might, however, be the occasion for a (venial) sin of sloth, lack of confidence in God, or unreasonable ambition for worldly success.

[41] *Ibid.,* Ia, q. 22, a. 1: "Ratio autem ordinandorum in finem proprie providentiae est. Est enim principalis pars prudentiae.... Et secundum hunc modum prudentia vel providentia Deo convenire potest."

[42] Cf. Many, *Praelectiones de Sacra Ordinatione,* p. 205; St. Thomas Aquinas, *Summa Theologica,* Ia, q. 22, a. 3: "... Deus immediate omnibus providet; quia in suo intellectu habet rationem omnium, etiam minimorum, et quascumque causas aliquibus effectibus praefecit, dedit eis virtutem ad illos effectus producendos."

[43] Cf. *Summa Theologica,* IIIa, q. 27, a. 4.

[44] Cf. *Comment. in Lib. IV Sent.* (*Opera Omnia,* ed. L. Vives, Paris, 1874), d. 24, q. 1, quaes. 5, solutio 1: "... ideo cuicumque datur potentia aliqua divinitus, dantur ea per quae executio illius potentiae

worthy to receive Orders is presupposed in him who is ordained, and accordingly this preparing grace is prior, both in the order of time and of causality, to the actual reception of the sacerdotal character by one who is divinely called.[45]

The canonist Many proposed a pertinent illustration for this doctrine when he compared the act of Providence selecting a future priest to the act of a human craftsman, who, when he desires to employ material for a specific purpose, adapts the material to the purpose for which it is intended.[46] This comparison clearly points out the distinction between the divine vocation itself and that complex of qualities which comprises fitness for the priesthood. The former is the cause, the latter is the effect. This distinction was insinuated by Gasparri when he defined a suitable ordinand as a person called by God *and* not impeded.[47]

---

potest congrue fieri ... ita in sacramento ordinis, per quod homo ordinatur ad aliorum sacramentorum dispensationem."

[45] Cf. St. Thomas Aquinas, *Summa Theologica*, Suppl., q. 35, a.1, ad 3um: "... praeexigitur gratia quae sufficiat ad hoc quod digne connumerentur in plebe Christi ...."

[46] Cf. *Praelectiones de Sacra Ordinatione*. p. 205.

[47] *De Sacra Ordinatione*, n. 109: "Igitur dici potest subjectum idoneum sacrae ordinationis esse personam vocatam a Deo, et non impeditam." Cf. Davis, *Moral and Pastoral Theology* (4. ed., 4 vols., London: Sheed and Ward, 1943), IV, 268: "... Divine Providence prepares future ministers for God's Church, by the bestowal on some select souls of certain qualities of character and certain special graces to fit them to embrace this state of life."

CHAPTER III

THE NECESSITY OF THE DIVINE VOCATION

ARTICLE 1. Basis of the Necessity

From the nature itself of the priesthood it is evident that the sacerdotal character is a certain participation in the fontal and supreme Priesthood of Jesus Christ. By the reception of Orders a priest is charged with the dignity of exercising his sacrificial and sacramental ministry in accordance with the end for which the Church was instituted, that is, the sanctification of others: *"sacerdos propter alios."* This is the radical significance of Gratian's dictum:

> Cetera enim sacramenta unicuique propter se dantur. . . . Istud solum non propter se solum, sed propter alios datur . . . ad quorum utilitatem, non solum ut presint, sed etiam ut prosint, sacerdotium datur.[1]

It is this quality of Orders—as most specially given for the spiritual benefit of the faithful—which imparts to the sacrament its uniquely quasi-charismatic nature.

The legally acknowledged divine purpose and character of the priesthood[2] at once suggests, in the manner of a conclusion, that one may not enter that office simply at his own will, but must receive an invitation from God, Whose ambassador he is[3] and under Whom he is to act as mediator in behalf of men. This obvious necessity for a divine vocation before one may licitly accept ordination has constantly furnished the legislation of the Church with matter for its disciplinary enactments calculated to deter from entrance into the sanctuary those who are devoid of the requisite call.[4]

[1] Ad C. 43, C. I, q. 1.

[2] Cf. Conc. Trident., sess. XXIII, *de ordine*, c. 2: "Cum autem divina res sit tam sancti sacerdotii ministerium . . . ."—Mansi, XXXIII, 138.

[3] II Cor., V, 20.

[4] Cf. Gasparri, *De Sacra Ordinatione*, n. 111.

ARTICLE 2. PRE-TRIDENTINE LAW

An examination of early canonical sources reveals a marked emphasis placed by the legislator on the need for divine vocation antecedent to ordination. Pope Leo the Great (440-461) advised the bishops of Africa to ascertain whether candidates possessed this vocation prior to the imposition of hands, lest the dignity of Orders be conferred contrary to divine law.[5] And in a parallel decree this Pontiff instructed prelates to be mindful that the Church can accept as *rectores* only those whom the Holy Spirit has specially singled out for the priesthood by divine activity in the order of grace: "*... dignatio coelestis gratiae gignat antistitem.*"[6]

Gregory the Great (590-604) in a letter to Bishop Siagrius of Autun (561-600), stated this norm to be observed in the choice of priests:

> In sacerdotibus ordinandis sinceritas vigeat; sit simplex et sine venalitate consensus: pura praeferatur electio, ut ad summam sacerdotii non suffragio venditorum provectus, sed Dei credatur iudicio esse.[7]

The phrase "*Dei credatur iudicio esse*" indicates that in the mind of the Pontiff the licit ordination of the candidate was the consequence of a divine judgment made antecedently to the reception of Orders. Such a necessary and pre-existing divine "judgment" seems tantamount to a vocation, and this conjecture is fortified when one examines an analogous epistle of Pope Leo, wherein bishops were warned of their accountability to God should they elevate to the priestly

[5] C. 13, D. LV; Jaffé, n. 410.

[6] *Sermo III*—Migne, *Patrologiae Cursus Completus, Series Latina* (221 vols., Parisiis, 1844-1855), LIV, 145 (hereafter cited *MPL*). Cf. a similar passage in Gregory the Great (590-604) in which this Pope comments on Osee VIII, 4: "*Ipsi regnaverunt, et non ex me ....*", applying this to those who enter the priesthood "*nequaquam divinitus vocati*", and by their cupidity "*culmen regiminis rapiunt potius quam assequuntur.*"—*Liber Regularis Pastoralis,* Pars I, c. 1—*MPL,* LXXVII, 14.

[7] C. 3, C. I, q. 6; Jaffé, n. 1747.

dignity someone of whose divine vocation they were in doubt. On the contrary, commendation was given to bishops who ordained only those aspirants whom they deemed divinely called.[8] This principle of the basic requirement of a God-given summons to Orders was placed in sharp relief by directives of Popes Innocent III (1198-1216)[9] and John XXII (1316-1334).[10]

ARTICLE 3. Doctrinal Evolution of the Necessity of the Divine Vocation—from the Council of Trent to the Present

The legislation of the Council of Trent on the Sacrament of Orders, on the reform of its discipline, and on the erection, the function and the support of ecclesiastical seminaries, provided considerable impetus to the development of the canonical doctrine of priestly vocation.

The Council had formulated its decrees in order to assure a suitable supply of worthy priests, and if its enactments had been accurately observed that desideratum would doubtlessly have been achieved. But the intention of the conciliar Fathers in this regard was not generally realized. Chaotic conditions during the post-"Reformation" period; political upheavals; lack of co-operation among the clergy to implement the Tridentine proposals, either because of indifference or inability to apply the remedies; the widespread persecution against the Church—all these and similar obstacles impeded the execution of the salutary measures recommended by the Council.

Consequent upon these unpropitious conditions, few semi-

[8] Cf. *Epistola XII—MPL,* LIV, 658. Cf. also Pope Gregory's relevant comment in *In Primum Regum Expositiones,* lib. V, c. 3, n. 2—*MPL,* LXXIX, 447, that God pre-elects His priests.

[9] Cf. c. 18, X, *de electione et electi potestate,* I, 6; Potthast, *Regesta Pontificum Romanorum inde ab anno post Christum natum 1198 ad annum 1304* (2 vols. in 1, Berolini, 1874-1875), n. 852 (hereafter cited Potthast).

[10] Cf. C. 1, *de electione,* tit. I, in Extravag. Ioan. XXII: "ad onus apostolicae servitutis superna dispositione vocati...."

naries were permanently established, and unworthy men entered the priesthood in too many instances with practically no formal training. In France, for example, of about twenty-five seminaries established between 1564 and 1620 (a small number for a Catholic nation) few were still in operation by the end of the first quarter of the seventeenth century.[11]

Since an effectual clergy depends upon an unceasing supply of suitable candidates, namely men divinely called to the sacred ministry, some canonists and moralists of this period devoted their efforts to an intensive study of the clerical vocation. Their purpose in the restatement and careful elaboration of the law requiring an antecedent God-given invitation to the priesthood was to preclude the unworthy—those not called—from seeking admission to Orders. These writers were evidently of the opinion that to insist on positive evidence of divine vocation was an effective means of deterring the unfit.

The first thorough and lucid treatment of the problem of divine vocation came from the pen of the French canonist-moralist Hallier (1595-1659), published in 1633. The position of this writer is succinctly set forth in this passage:

> Congruum igitur est ut nemo sacris initietur ordinibus, nisi quem secreta saltem voce Deus ad ministerium invitarit . . . . quis vero legitime potest Deo ministrare, nisi a Deo electus fuerit? . . . non est verus apostolus Christi, nisi qui per voluntatem Dei constitutus, nisi qui non ab hominibus, neque per hominem, sed per Jesum Christum renuntiatus; nisi qui a Deo vocatus segregatusque fuerit.[12]

This insistence on the necessity of the divine calling before one might lawfully advance to ordination—that necessity is pointed out five times in this passage—reflected the mind

[11] Cf. Hallier (1595-1659), *De Sacris Electionibus et Ordinationibus ex Antiquo et Novo Ecclesiae Usu* (in J.P. Migne, *Theologiae Cursus Completus*, Vol. XXIV, Parisiis, 1860), Pars I, sect. I, cap. II, n. 15 (hereafter cited Hallier); Blowick, *Priestly Vocation* (Dublin: M.H. Gill and Son, Ltd., 1932), pp. 8-9.

[12] Hallier, Pars I, sect. III, cap. II, n. 21.

of other authors of the post-Tridentine era, notably the adherents of the founder of the Sulpicians, Jean Jacques Olier (1608-1657).[13]

A perusal of the more notable decretalists during the two centuries subsequent to the Council of Trent discloses that they made no direct reference to the doctrine of divine vocation. Their treatments were restricted to the frame of jurisprudence provided by the *Corpus Iuris Canonici* and the Tridentine decrees. However, these writers did explore all the elements later considered by legalists as essentially constitutive of vocation, but they did not refer expressly to the concept implied in the phrase "divine vocation."[14]

Thomassinus (1619-1695) studied the necessity of vocation in his treatment of the law of benefices, and taught that the divine invitation must always precede ordination. In condemning the abuses inherent in the accepting of the priesthood without the proper motive, he stated: *"Explodendi protinus sunt, quos terrena cupiditas, non divina vocatio clero inseruit."*[15] And in a cognate text, wherein this author likened the vocation given to mere men with that given to Christ, appeared the conclusion that the necessity of a vocation for lawful ordination is rooted in an unvarying and inviolable juridical principle.[16]

Van Espen (1646-1728) was another canonist who developed briefly but pointedly the same teaching as Thomassinus. He introduced the matter of vocation in his study of

[13] Cf. Olier's *Traité des Saintes Ordres* (Migne, *Oeuvres Completes*, Paris, 1856); Abelly (1603-1691), *Sacerdos Christianus* (Vesontione, 1838); Branchereau (1819-1913), *De La Vocation Sacerdotale* (Paris, 1896).

[14] Cf. Barbosa (1589-1649), *De Officio et Potestate Episcopi* (Lugduni, 1656), Pars II, alleg. II, nn. 6, 7; Fagnanus (1598-1678), *Commentaria in Quinque Libros Decretalium* (5 vols. in 3, Coloniae Allobrogum, 1759), Lib. I, tit. XI; Reiffenstuel (1642-1703), *Jus Canonicum Universum* (5 vols. in 7, Parisiis, 1864-1870), Lib. I, tit. XI; Schmalzgrueber (1663-1735), *Jus Ecclesiasticum Universum* (5 vols. in 12, Romae, 1843-1845), Lib. I, tit. XI.

[15] Pars II, lib. I, cap. XXV, n. 8.

[16] Pars II, lib. II, cap. I, n. 1.

the discipline governing the constitution of those benefices which for their incumbents involved the care of souls, and this writer was of the opinion that one may not accept the care of souls unless one has evidently been divinely called to such an office for which he is duly qualified.[17]

St. Alphonsus Liguori (1696-1787) perpetuated this teaching when he insisted on the requirement of divine vocation as something antecedent to the ecclesiastical summons. This renowned Doctor accurately differentiated between the two calls, the internal and the external, and registered surprise that so few commentators had previously examined the vocational problem.[18]

The requirement of positive evidence of divine vocation as a prerequisite to licit ordination became well-accepted canonical doctrine before the end of the nineteenth century. Wernz (1842-1914) in his treatment of Orders prefaced the consideration of the qualities to be looked for in a candidate by declaring that the presence of a true divine vocation in the ordinand is of primary importance.[19] Virtually all modern canonists are of the same opinion.[20]

[17] *Jus Ecclesiasticum Universum* (Venetiis, 1769), Tit. V, cap. I, n. 11: "... num [quispiam] ad curam animarum a Deo fit vocatus: signaque tam internae, quam externae vocationis pro rei magnitudine discusserit: quin et intima conscientiae scrutatus sit, an ad curam animarum non *proprii* commodi, aut vanae gloriae intuitu: sed ad promovendam Dei gloriam, et salutem animarum procurandam unice moveatur."

[18] Cf. *Theologia Moralis* (4 vols., ed. cura et studio P. Leonardi Gaudé, Romae: Typis Polyglottis Vaticanis, 1905-1912), Lib. VI, n. 802.

[19] *Ius Decretalium* (3. ed., 6 vols., Prati, 1913-1915), Vol. II, pars I, n. 85: "... ipse Deus ministros altaris novi testamenti ex omni gente et tribu sibi evocet, imprimis ordinandus praeditus sit oportet vera vocatione divina ...."

[20] Cf. Gasparri (1852-1934), *De Sacra Ordinatione*, n. 110; Many (†1922), *Praelectiones de Sacra Ordinatione*, pp. 203 sqq.; Cappello, *Tractatus Canonico-Moralis de Sacramentis*, Vol. II, Pars III (*De Sacra Ordinatione*), n. 363; Coronata, *Institutiones Iuris Canonici, De Sacramentis* (3 vols., Taurini-Romae: Marietti, 1943-1946), II, n. 48 (hereafter cited *De Sacramentis*); Regatillo, *Ius Sacramentarium* (2 vols., Santander: Sal Terrae, 1945-1946), II, n. 72; Wernz-Vidal, *Ius*

Vermeersch (1858-1936), on the contrary, while allowing for the fact of divine vocation, identified it with the ecclesiastical call extended by the authorities of the Church. In keeping with this opinion, no antecedent call from God is needed since the totality of the vocational concept is included in the bishop's summons to Orders followed by the ordination itself.[21]

ARTICLE 4. JURIDICAL ENACTMENTS RELATIVE TO THE NECESSITY OF THE DIVINE VOCATION—FROM THE COUNCIL OF TRENT TO THE PRESENT

In its twenty-third session, devoted to reforms of discipline in regard to the Sacrament of Orders, the Council of Trent took cognizance of the essentiality of divine vocation when it labeled as "thieves" and "robbers" those who entered Sacred Orders temerariously.[22] The signification of the phrase *"propria temeritate sibi sumunt"* used by the Council, can be gauged from the force of the scriptural reference[23] wherein the parallel idea of unlawful entry is expressed. This passage is frequently pointed out by exegetes and by canonists as demonstrative of the source and necessity of the divine vocation.[24] He alone who goes into the sheepfold

---

Canonicum, IV, n. 216; Pruemmer, *Manuale Iuris Canonici* (6. ed. Friburgi-Brisgoviae: Herder, 1933), q. 320; Beste, *Introductio in Codicem* (Collegeville, Minn.: St. John's Abbey Press, 1938), p. 517.

[21] Vermeersch-Creusen, *Epitome Iuris Canonici* (5. ed., 3 vols., Mechlinae: H. Dessain, 1933-1936), II, n. 242: "... actio vocantis Dei et Superioris ecclesiastici in recto ponitur ...."; Vermeersch, *Religious and Ecclesiastical Vocation* (translated from the Latin by Joseph G. Kempf, St. Louis: Herder, 1925), p. 69: "By the will of God, *consequent* to their external acceptance, those are called to the priesthood who lawfully receive Holy Orders." Throughout the present dissertation, the phrase "ecclesiastical vocation" is uniformly used in the sense of the external call from the Church, although it may properly be used also to signify the divine call.

[22] *De ordine*, c. 4: "... qui ea propria temeritate sibi sumunt, omnes non ecclesiae ministros, sed fures et latrones per ostium non ingressos habendos esse."—Mansi, XXXIII, 139.

[23] John, X, 1.

[24] Cf. *supra*, Chap. II, *Article I*.

by the door—which is Christ—can be considered as a legitimate shepherd of the Lord's flock. An analysis of this notion provides the inference that it was the intent of the conciliar decree to shut the door of the sanctuary to one presuming to intrude therein upon his own authority.

Now, assuredly the Tridentine decree here involved cannot be supposed to envision the almost inconceivable situation of a person who succeeds in receiving Orders without having previously been accepted for them by ecclesiastical authority! Such a supposititious instance would be where one fraudulently places himself among the ranks of the *ordinandi* just before the actual ordination, and is ordained with them despite the lack of any canonical summons. To reason that the decree of the Council was predicated upon this remote possibility would be entirely unwarranted in the absence of some indication to that effect in the decree itself. Hence the conclusion is imposed that the phrase *"propria temeritate sibi sumunt"* has reference to the temerity inherent in the acceptation of Orders without a divine call to them.[25]

This reasoning is confirmed by a correlation with an allied admonitory text of the Catechism of the Council of Trent:

DIVINE CALL

> Let no one *take the honour to himself, but he that is called by God as Aaron was* (Heb. V, 4); and they are called by God who are called by the lawful ministers of His Church. It is to those who arrogantly intrude themselves into this ministry that the Lord must be understood to refer when He says: *I did not send prophets, yet they ran* (Jer. XXIII, 21). Nothing can be more unhappy and

[25] Cf. Wernz-Vidal, *Ius Canonicum,* IV, n. 216: "Conc. vero Trid. dicit fures et latrones per ostium non ingressos habendos esse, qui *'haec ministeria propria temeritate sibi sumunt'*; at qui [quo?] fieri potest ut assumantur sine vocatione canonica? Alia ergo admittenda est, ideoque divina."

wretched than such a class of men as this, and nothing more calamitous to the Church of God.[26]

Pope Sixtus V (1585-1590), a Pontiff known for his strict enforcement of the disciplinary decrees of the Tridentine Council, pointedly noted the Church's insistence on the necessity of the antecedent divine vocation in his Constitution *Sanctum et salutare* of January 5, 1589. In this document the Pontiff excoriated those who, although unworthy and incapable of the priestly office, nevertheless entered upon it, and these he described as led on by the wiles of the devil rather than by the holy calling of God.[27]

Pope Innocent XIII (1721-1724) in addressing the Spanish hierarchy called the attention of the ordinaries to their obligation of accepting for the priesthood only aspirants who *"in sortem Domini vocati sunt."*[28] Benedict XIV (1740-1758) employed phraseology of the same import,[29] and it was concerning the proper clerical formation of all those who were "called to the lot of the Lord" that Pope Pius IX (1846-1878) wrote to the bishops throughout the world.[30]

[26] *Catechism of The Council of Trent for Parish Priests* (ed. by J.A. McHugh and C.J. Callan, New York, 1923), *The Sacrament of Holy Orders*, pp. 318-319.

[27] § 1: "Cum enim multi etiam interdum inhabiles, et indigni, non vocati sancta Dei vocatione, sed potius Satanae dolis decepti, praetextu devotionis, et pietatis, rem quidem sacram, et divinum munus, intempestive tamen, et inordinate affectantes, seu temporale aliquod commodum, aut lucrum sibi proponentes . . . temere se ingerant."—*Codicis Iuris Canonici Fontes* (cura Emi Petri Card. Gasparii editi, 9 vols., Romae [postea Civitate Vaticana]: Typis Polyglottis Vaticanis, 1923-1939. Vols. VII-IX ed. cura et studio Emi Iustiniani Card. Serédi), n. 166 (hereafter cited *Fontes*).

[28] Const. *Apostolici ministerii*, 23 maii 1723—*Fontes*, n. 280.

[29] Cf. ep. encycl. *Ubi primum*, 3 dec. 1740, § 2—*Fontes*, n. 304.

[30] Ep. encycl. *Qui pluribus*, 9 nov. 1846, § 8: ". . . in sortem Domini vocatos."—*Fontes*, n. 504. Cf. also Pius IX's allocut. *Quibus luctuosissimis*, 5 sept. 1851, § 3—*Fontes*, n. 512; S.C. de Prop. Fide, instr. (ad Vic. Ap. Sin.), 18 oct. 1883, § 4, n. 4: "Districte vero praecipit S. Consilium ut in maius Seminarium (*grand séminaire*), ubi erectum sit, nullimode admittantur laici; qui vero vocatione ecclesiastica carere

Pope Leo XIII (1878-1903) in an encyclical to the clergy of France incisively pointed out the position of the Church regarding the indispensability of a divine vocation ontologically prior (and prior in causality) to the ecclesiastical summons to Orders. This Pontiff declared that since no state was so elevated, difficult and dignified as the Catholic priesthood, therefore no precaution ought to be omitted to insure the worthy preparation of those whom Providence singles out for the clerical life. He stressed the primordial importance of discerning in candidates the presence of a germinal God-given vocation before the issuance of any external call to Orders by the hierarchy.[31]

In 1900 Leo XIII promulgated the decrees of the Plenary Council of Latin America which had convened the preceding year. Several sections of its conciliar acts are of singular clarity in respect to the prescription of the Church demanding sufficient indication of a divine calling in the subject of sacred ordination. Thus the words:

---

dignoscantur, statim ab eo excludantur ita ut de tali collegio verissime dici possit *illud Dei ministrorum perpetuum seminarium esse.*"—*Fontes*, n. 4903; S.C. Ep. et Reg., instr. (ad Ep. Hungariae), 28 maii 1896, § 2: "Episcopi autem, memores gravissimae Apostoli admonitionis: *manus cito nemini imposueris, neque communicaveris peccatis alienis*, summa cum diligentia explorent num forte sint qui, non vocati a Deo, seipsos sive ob quaestum sive ob ambitionem terrenamque quamcumque cupiditatem ad sacerdotium ecclesiasticumque ministerium intrudant . . . ."—*Fontes*, n. 2030; S.C.C., decr. *Vetuit*, 22 dec. 1905 —*Fontes*, n. 4327.

[31] Cf. ep. encycl. *Depuis le jour*, 8 sept. 1899, § § 6, 7: "Rien donc ne devra être négligé pour préparer à remplir dignement et fructueusement une telle mission, ceus qu'une vocation divine y appelle. Avant toute chose, il convient de discerner, parmi les jeunes enfants, ceus en qui le Très-Haut a déposé le germe d'une semblable vocation."—*Fontes*, n. 642. Cf. also this Pope's letter, *Officio sanctissimo*, 22 dec. 1877, § 8: "Omnino oportet et necesse est habere eos [sacerdotes] sibi persuasum ac prope insculptum in animis, se iam non de saeculi esse consortione, at vero Dei consilio electos esse, qui, in communione saeculi aetatem agentes, vitam tamen Christi Domini vivant."—*Fontes*, n. 596.

> Cum sacrorum ministri probi et vere idonei, Dei donum sint, et sane maximum, hinc, in electione promovendorum ad Ordines, ante omnia enixe rogandus est idem Deus ... ut huiusmodi *operarios mittat in messem suam* (Luc. X, 2) ....[32]

describe worthy ministers as a gift of God and their mission as a consequence of His providential act in the order of grace. Their final lawful elevation to Orders presupposes the anterior divine selection:

> Venerandam clericalis status atque sacerdotii dignitatem et honorem nemo sibi sumat, nisi qui vocatur a Deo, tamquam Aaron (Heb. V, 4). Domini enim est eligere quos vult esse suos, suorumque mysteriorum dispensatores.[33]

A. THE ROMAN DECISION

Despite the consistently reiterated doctrine relative to the requirement of divine vocation and its formulation in the canonical prescriptions hitherto considered, a French seminary professor, Canon Joseph Lahitton, published in 1909 a book entitled *La Vocation Sacerdotale*.[34] In treating other matters pertinent to the problem of vocation this author declared that no special divine call was required for licit ordination, that antecedent divine vocation was a fiction since the *totality* of the vocational concept consisted in the episcopal invitation to Orders. His stand was novel and provocative.[35]

Consequent upon the appearance of this work of Lahitton a heated controversy sprang up among canonists and moralists. It centered upon the question of the reality of the anterior vocation and its necessity for the lawful recep-

[32] *Acta et Decreta Concilii Plenarii Americae Latinae* (Romae: Typis Vaticanis, 1902), tit. V—*De Sacramentis*, cap. VII, n. 577. Cf. also *ibid.*, n. 579: "... num a Deo legitime vocati ...."

[33] *Op. cit.*, tit. VII—*De Institutione Clericorum*, cap. I, n. 606.

[34] Nouvelle édit., Paris, 1913; 2. ed., Paris, 1928.

[35] Cf. *La Vocation Sacerdotale, passim.* Cf. also Vermeersch, *Religious and Ecclesiastical Vocation*, pp. 74-83, for his favorable support of Lahitton.

tion of Orders. The dispute re-echoed in Rome where it was deemed of sufficient weight to occupy the study of a special commission of Cardinals under the presidency of the noted Cardinal Merry del Val (1865-1930). By a cautiously-worded approval of particular sections of Lahitton's book, delivered on July 2, 1912, this Commission neither expressly affirmed nor expressly denied the existence and essentiality of the antecedent divine vocation. Rather the judgment concerned itself with three other propositions found in the work of the French author.[36]

Some commentators have understood the decision of the Commission as supporting the opinion of Lahitton,[37] but this interpretation seems unwarranted by the tenor of the decree,[38] and subsequent pontifical acts have made that interpretation even less tenable. For example, two weeks after the promulgation of the Commission's decision, the Sacred Consistorial Congregation authoritatively adverted to the antecedent vocation as an interior and necessary thing: a grace.[39]

[36] *AAS*, IV (1912), 485.

[37] Cf. Vermeersch, *Epitome Iuris Canonici*, II, n. 242, § 3: "Voluntate Dei *consequente* ipsam externam assumptionem, vocantur quotquot rite assumpti sunt ab Ecclesia, cui delectus sacerdotum commissa est." The same idea is expressed in his *Religious and Ecclesiastical Vocation*, p. 69: "By the will of God, *consequent* to their external acceptance, those are called to the priesthood who lawfully receive Holy Orders." Cf. also Blowick, *Priestly Vocation*, pp. 114-116. This writer interpreted the judgment of the Commission as if it positively precluded the concept of a special and antecedent divine vocation.

[38] Cf. Cappello, *Tractatus Canonico-Moralis de Sacramentis*, II, Pars III (*De Sacra Ordinatione*), n. 374: "Inde minime sequitur (ex decisione Commissionis), ut nonnulli immerito affirmant, vocationem divinam non requiri, proindeque admissionem ab Episcopo constituere ipsam vocationem sacerdotalem seu cum ea identificari. Sunt res omnino distinctae." Cf. also canonists cited *supra*, Chap. IV, *Article* 3.

[39] Litt. circ., S.C.C., 16 iul. 1912: "Ma checchè ne sia di ciò, poichè per le divine promesse è certo che mai si inaridirà in Israele la stirpe levitica, e che l'assistenza divina e le vocazioni allo stato ecclesiastico non mancheranno nella Chiesa *usque ad consummationem saeculi*, nè faranno giammai difetto anime generose che rispondano alla voce del Signore . . . ."—*AAS*, IV (1912), 492.

B. THE LAW OF THE CODE

The Code itself embodies the purport of many previous enactments of ecclesiastical law when it formulates this norm in canon 1353:

> Dent operam sacerdotes, praesertim parochi, ut pueros, qui indicia praebeant ecclesiasticae vocationis, peculiaribus curis a saeculi contagiis arceant, ad pietatem informent, primis litterarum studiis imbuant divinaeque in eis vocationis germen foveant.

It is significant that this canon incorporates two phrases referring to the fact of a vocation as something divinely implanted in the souls of young men. This double use of "*vocatio*", viewed in the context of the canon, indicates that the intent of the law is that only youths who reveal positive signs of a divine invitation should be encouraged to seek ordination.

This interpretation is further strengthened by its correlation with canon 1357, § 2, which requires a bishop frequently to visit the diocesan seminary the better to ascertain the probable vocation of diocesan seminarians. This obligation becomes of increasing urgency as the day of ordination draws near. The more proximate the moment for the bishop's issuance of the call to Orders, the more imperative is it that he have moral certitude[40] that the ordinand has indeed been divinely chosen for the sacerdotal state.

Directives emanating from the Holy See subsequent to the promulgation of the Code of Canon Law have, in keeping with the Code's provisions, repeatedly urged those who are entrusted with the formation of future priests to discover in youths evidence of a vocation and to admit only such into the seminary.[41] On December 27, 1930, the Sacred Congre-

[40] Canon 973, § 3: "Episcopus sacros ordines nemini conferat quin ex positivis argumentis moraliter certus sit de eius canonica idoneitate; secus non solum gravissime peccat, sed etiam periculo sese committit alienis communicandi peccatis."

[41] Cf. Pius XI, ep. (ad Archiepiscopum Caracensem, 25 apr. 1923): "Itaque id primum omnium, venerabiles fratres, efficite, ut quibus in adulescentulis divinae vocationis semina deprehenderitis, ii non modo

gation of the Sacraments issued an instruction to all ordinaries. It began with a forcible statement in reference to the extreme danger in store for the Church and the faithful when men devoid of a true divine vocation are permitted to receive ordination: *"Quam ingens Ecclesiae atque animarum saluti detrimentum inferant qui, divina destituti vocatione, sacerdotale ministerium inire praesumunt, angelicis ipsis humeris formidandum, neminem profecto fugit."*[42] The sole purpose of this instruction was to insure a diligent examination of candidates for the priesthood in order to exclude those who lack the requisite calling.[43]

---

ad pietatem accuratius informentur, sed etiam in Seminaria dioecesana quamprimum excipiantur."—*AAS*, XV (1923), 276.

[42] Instr. *Quam ingens*, § 1—*AAS*, XXIII (1931), 120.

[43] Cf. *loc. cit.*: "Unde qui a Spiritu Sancto sunt positi regere Ecclesiam Dei, ad plurima atque ingentia avertenda mala ab ipsa Ecclesia atque a christifidelibus, sedulissimam adhibeant curam oportet, ne tanti ministerii aditus illis pateat, quibus, ob defectum sacerdotalis vocationis, aptandum est illud Christi Domini: 'Amen, amen dico vobis: qui non intrat per ostium in ovile ovium sed ascendit aliunde, ille fur est et latro' (Ioann., X, 1) . . . aperte [sacerdotes] ostendunt, se fuisse praepostero modo in sacram militiam adlectos, seu non satis fuisse exploratam vocationem . . . ." Cf. also Pius XI, ep. encycl. *Ad catholici sacerdotii fastigium*, 20 dec. 1935, § 3: "Quamobrem ipsamet, Numinis instinctu ducta, Seminaria esse ubicumque gentium instituenda decernit, in quibus singulari cura sacri ordinis alumni educentur."—*AAS*, XXVIII (1936), 37; Pius XII, sermo, 24 iun. 1939: ". . . Omnipotenti Deo gratias agamus pro hac divinae vocationis plenitudine . . . ."—*AAS*, XXXI (1939), 245; Pius XII, motu propr. *Cum Nobis*, 4 nov. 1941—*AAS*, XXXIII (1941), 479; Pius XII, ep. ap. *Haud mediocrem*, 22 nov. 1941—*AAS*, XXXIV (1942), 234; Pius XII, ep. ap. *Volvidos cinco anos*, 23 apr. 1947—*AAS*, XXXIX (1947), 286-287. The last two documents were directed to the bishops of Bolivia and Brazil respectively.

PART II

THE ECCLESIASTICAL VOCATION TO THE PRIESTHOOD

CHAPTER I

THE NATURE OF THE ECCLESIASTICAL VOCATION

In virtue of the sacerdotal character indelibly impressed upon his soul at ordination[1] a priest is enabled to fulfill an intercessory office between God and men. This function of mediation exercised by the power of Orders imparts to the sacred priesthood a religio-social nature, since God has deigned to effect man's salvation ordinarily by the grace conveyed through the instrumentality of the Church's sacramental system.

By divine institution the continuity of both the Church and its sacramental life is secured in the existence and activity of a twofold hierarchy: that of Orders and that of jurisdiction.[2] The powers incident upon membership in these hierarchies are similar in essence, for both are specified by the same ultimate end, the salvation of souls. But they differ inasmuch as the power of Orders accompanies the priestly character inhering accidentally in the soul of the ordained, while the power of jurisdiction results from a moral and social relation existing between superior and subject. Moreover, these powers are unlike in the sense that the sacramental character of Orders is not exposed to loss or diminution, while jurisdiction, dependent immediately upon the human will for its efficacy, remains in itself revocable and liable to curtailment.[3]

Although the power of Orders and the power of jurisdiction are intimately associated under the Church's present

[1] Canon 732, § 1.

[2] Canons 108, § 3; 109.

[3] Cf. Wernz-Vidal, *Ius Canonicum,* II, n. 48.

discipline,[4] nevertheless they are essentially distinct and separable. This truth is plain in the case of a titular bishop, or also conceivably in the supposition of a layman's election to the papacy: in the former instance there is frequently realized the power of Orders without actual ordinary jurisdiction; in the latter (remote) possibility there would be actual jurisdiction without the power of Orders.[5]

It is the vocation solely to the power of Orders that is accurately connoted with the phrase "priestly vocation", rather than the summons to a participation in jurisdictional power which frequently, but not necessarily, is associated with a priest's sacramental functions.

Because of the already mentioned religio-social character of the sacred priesthood, no one may lawfully accept ordination if he has not been invited to it by both God and the Church. Hence if one receives the priesthood without a divine-internal vocation and without an ecclesiastical-external call, a usurpation would thus ensue. No one may licitly discharge a mediatory function without the mutual consent of the terms of that mediation.[6] Such an inordinate assumption of the priesthood would constitute a nonobservance of the design of Providence, which has established the Church as a divine-human society.[7]

[4] Cf. canon 118: "Soli clerici possunt potestatem sive ordinis sive iurisdictionis ecclesiasticae et beneficia ac pensiones ecclesiasticas obtinere."

[5] For an analysis of the relationship between the two powers, cf. Ryan, *Principles of Episcopal Jurisdiction*, The Catholic University of America Canon Law Studies, n. 120 (Washington, D.C.: The Catholic University of America Press, 1939), p. 12, and *passim*. Cf. also Gasparri, *De Sacra Ordinatione*, n. 20. In earlier times the distinction between Orders and jurisdiction, and their possible separability from each other were less apparent than in later centuries because up to the 12th century the act of ordination coincided temporally with the granting of jurisdiction as deriving through an act of election or the bestowal of the canonical mission.—Cf. Wernz-Vidal, *Ius Canonicum*, II, n. 48, footnote.

[6] Gasparri, *De Sacra Ordinatione*, n. 111.

[7] Cf. canon 100, § 1; Cappello, *Summa Iuris Publici Ecclesiastici*, n. 81. But the degree of moral culpability in the usurpation would be commensurate with the degree of one's awareness of non-vocation.

The invitation given by the Church to Orders is accordingly no less imperative for a lawful ordination than is the antecedent divine vocation electing and preparing one for the priesthood. For this reason, vocation—on the part of the Church—can be defined as an act predicated on the Church's supernatural mission, by which ecclesiastical authority summons to Orders those individuals whom it judges divinely called to Orders.

The actual choice of its ministers is specifically an employment of the Church's jurisdictional power,[8] and the normal outcome of that selection, as realized in the conferring of the sacerdotal character, is properly an exercise of the plenitude of the power of Orders. Inasmuch as the Church justly vindicates to itself a plenary and exclusive spiritual authority divinely entrusted to it by its Founder,[9] it accordingly enjoys the unrestricted right of selecting as ministers of cult whomsoever it chooses, and peremptorily disallows any infringement upon this prerogative.[10]

[8] Cf. Cappello, *op. cit.*, n. 139.

[9] Cf. Cappello, *op. cit.*, n. 81: "Societas a Christo D. instituta, ut in ea et per eam exclusive homines vitam aeternam consequantur."

[10] Cf. canon 109; Conc. Trident., sess. XXIII, *de ordine*, c. 4—Mansi, XXXIII, 139.

CHAPTER II

THE SOURCE OF THE ECCLESIASTICAL VOCATION

ARTICLE 1. The Relation of Election to Ordination

As a public moral person the Church, in its nature of a supreme and sovereign society, can bring its powers to bear only through the medium of duly constituted representatives, and so in its capacity of serving mankind as a conduit of divine grace, truth and law, the Church must make use of the services of certain of its members to conduct its sacramental system, its teaching function and its rule.[1]

Residential bishops are in a particular manner the authorized representatives of the Church in the dioceses of which they are the chief Pastors. And they are members of the ecclesiastical hierarchy in the strictest acceptation of that term, for by their very office they possess perfect authority both in the internal and in the external forums. Thus their legislative, judicial and coercive powers are truly ordinary.[2]

From the inception of the Church bishops have consistently exerted a notable influence in the selection and final acceptance of candidates for Holy Orders. But the scope of this influence as well as its universal acceptance have not always been accorded the plenary and unquestioned juridical recognition reflected in the present canonical provisions.[3] A brief historical survey of the evolutionary development of this discipline will aid in the clarification of the concept of the episcopal call as well as facilitate the interpretation and the application of contemporary legislation regulating it.

Because of the intimate connection between the power of

[1] Cf. Cappello, *op. cit.*, n. 85: "Itaque omnia adsunt elementa, quibus Ecclesia Christi ut *vera societas* constituitur, et quidem *externa* et *visibilis:* societas, inquam, non modo hominum cum Deo, sed et hominum inter se mutuo colligatorum, nimirum societas *iuridica, publica, hierarchica,* etc." (Italics are Cappello's.)

[2] Cf. canons 329; 334; 335, § 1; Cappello, *op. cit.*, n. 349.

[3] Cf. canons 968, § 1; 969, § 1; 973, § 3.

jurisdiction and the power of Orders readily observable in the pristine canonical sources,[4] one frequently discovers that the summons to ordination was identified with the election to a participation in ecclesiastical jurisdiction.[5] This identification was especially likely when one was elevated directly from the lay state to the episcopacy, but in every instance wherein an office demanded an ordained incumbent, his subsequent ordination (if not previously had) was hardly distinguished from his election. Thus the actual conferment of Orders was often in effect tantamount to a ratification of the election to the office that required ordination.[6]

Because of this close bond between promotion to office and ordination, the question of ecclesiastical elections is certainly relevant to the question of ecclesiastical vocation. The Church has invariably tried to safeguard the beneficial dispensing of sacramental power against abuse by entrusting it only to those who were duly elected to office that postulated its exercise. And the aim of the legislation in governing the conduct of elections was to guarantee that only suitable subjects—divinely called to the ministry—were ordained. Thus election to an office entailing a *cura animarum* became a practical and tangible test of a candidate's vocation and fitness for the duties of the priesthood.

ARTICLE 2. THE HISTORICAL BACKGROUND OF ELECTION

The choice of Matthias for the priesthood by means of the casting of lots[7] was a residuary custom that had remained from the age of the Jewish synagogue. It was not calculated to serve as a future norm for the Christian Church in the calling of its priests. Thomassinus interpreted this mode of

[4] Cf. Kirch, *Enchiridion Fontium Historiae Ecclesiasticae Antiquae* (4. ed., Friburgi-Brisgoviae, 1923), n. 10.

[5] Cf. Wernz-Vidal, *Ius Canonicum,* II, n. 48 (footnote): "... fere usque ad saeculum duodecimum simul *eodem tempore,* quo per electionem vel missionem canonicam *iurisdictio* data est, etiam *ordinatio* fuit peracta."

[6] Cf. c. 13, D. LXIII; Mansi, XV, 601.

[7] Acts, I, 26.

selection as a consequence of the Apostles' conviction that, since Christ had directly chosen the other Apostles, it was therefore fitting that the Holy Spirit control the selection of a successor for the apostate Judas, and divine activity would presumably play a major role in a determination made by the casting of lots.[8]

Although it is not established precisely what influence the body of the faithful had in the choice of priests during the first century of the Church, still it seems fairly certain that they enjoyed some sort of elective right. This is evident from an instruction to the members of the infant Church by Pope Clement I (91-99) about the year 96. The Pontiff warned the Christians to choose as their spiritual leaders only those who were worthy for the ministry by reason of their excellent character.[9]

After the close of the Apostolic Age the selection of a bishop was performed by other bishops of the same ecclesiastical province in the presence of the faithful and the clergy, who together possessed a consultative vote. The definitive decision as to the acceptance or rejection of a candidate was reserved to the body of the provincial bishops, who themselves issued the ecclesiastical vocation.[10] In the choice of an aspirant for the simple priesthood the discipline was analogous,[11] for in that case also the decisive invitation to Orders came from the ordinary, although the counsel and

[8] Pars II, lib. II, cap. I, n. 1.

[9] Cf. Kirch, *Enchiridion Fontium Historiae Ecclesiasticae Antiquae*, n. 10.

[10] Cf. Hefele, *Histoire des Conciles* (translated from the 2nd German edition by H. Leclercq, 10 vols. in 19, Paris: Letouzey et Ané, 1907-1938), I, 547 (hereafter cited Hefele), and also the (pseudo-Isidorian) decree of Pope Anacletus (76-88) in Epis. II, *De ordinatione episcoporum et omnium clericorum*—Migne, *Patrologiae Cursus Completus, Series Graeca* (161 vols., Parisiis, 1857-1866), II, 802: "... sacerdotes a proprio ordinentur episcopo, ita ut cives et alii sacerdotes assensum praebeant...."

[11] Cf. the instruction of Pope Siricius (384-398): "... presbyterium vel episcopatum, si eum cleri ac plebis edecumarit electio."—*MPL*, XIII, 1143; Jaffé, n. 385.

approbation of the clergy and the laity (the *fraternitas*) were of considerable weight.[12] It was the opinion of Hefele (1809-1893) that the testimony and consent of the *fraternitas* frequently decided *de facto,* if not *de iure,* which candidate would obtain an office, and thus also the ordination demanded by it.[13]

A letter allegedly written by St. Cyprian (†258) is substantiative of the position of Hefele, for it admitted that the people enjoyed a certain power to reject unworthy candidates and to indicate which had their approval.[14] This method of selecting the clergy became the crystallized practice by the time of the Council of Ancyra (314), which restricted itself to a restatement and confirmation of the above-mentioned procedure.[15] The I Ecumenical Council of Nicaea (325) made no provision for the elective voice of the *fraternitas,* but likewise did not exclude it. This omission of any reference to the established practice indicated at least the Council's tolerance of the prevailing custom.[16] A canon of the reputed IV Council of Carthage (398) positively required bishops to seek the advice and to obtain the acquiescence of the *fraternitas* prior to the ordination of priests.[17] Councils of the fourth century appear to have acknowledged the discretionary power of the *fraternitas* as an accepted legal institution, for there was no intimation of any intention to exclude that power even in the very

[12] C. 119, C. 1, q. 1; Jaffé, n. 1253.

[13] Cf. Hefele, *loc. cit.;* c. 11, D. LXIII; Jaffé, n. 663.

[14] *Epistola LXVII—Corpus Scriptorum Ecclesiasticorum Latinorum* (Editum consilio et impensis Academiae Litterarum Caesareae Vindobonensis, Vindobonae: Apud Geroldi Filium, 1866—), III, (2), 737.

[15] Cf. Mansi, II, 521.

[16] Cf. Hefele, I, 539.

[17] C. 5, D. XXIV: "Episcopus sine consilio clericorum suorum non ordinet, ita ut civium conniventium et testimonium querat."—Hefele, III, 111. Thomassinus explained that the testimony of the "fraternity" was so cogent for this reason: *"Multa fallunt episcopos, quae plebem non fallunt . . . nihil effugere potest oculos, auresque, et conscientiam innumerabilis multitudinis . . . ."*—Pars II, lib. II, cap. I, n. 3.

canons where such an exclusion might well have been indicated.[18]

While the role of the faithful in the selection of the clergy had diminished in importance in the Eastern Church by the fifth century, probably due to abuses, it was nevertheless preserved for yet several centuries in the Western Church.[19]

In those instances where the early canonical sources have reference to the ecclesiastical vocation to the priesthood (as contrasted with the election to the episcopal office), it is indicated that the ordinary of the diocese wherein a priest was to exercise his ministry possessed the exclusive right and obligation of selecting candidates. Thus Pope Leo I (440-461) in a letter to the bishops of Africa exhorted them to exercise extreme care in admitting aspirants to Orders, warning the ordinaries of the grave danger implied in the hasty imposition of hands, and placing upon their shoulders the full responsibility for the choice of worthy ministers.[20] The legislation contained in Decretal and post-Decretal law did not, indeed, deny the existence of authority in others than the ordinary, but their capacity in the matter of ecclesiastical vocation was regularly restricted to a consultative function.[21]

[18] Cf. the Council of Antioch (341), canon XIX—Bruns, I, 85; the Council of Sardica (343), canon VI—Bruns, I, 93; the Council of Laodicea (343/381), canon XIII—Bruns, I, 74. The *Codex Ecclesiae Africanae* (Bruns, I, 162) and c. 1, D. LXIV, repeated the parallel text of the Nicaean Council—Hefele, I, 539.

[19] Cf. Gratian's rubric to c. 8, D. LXIII: "His omnibus auctoritatibus laici excluduntur ab electione sacerdotum . . . ."; Hefele, I, 547; Van Espen, *Jus Ecclesiasticum Universum*, Pars I, tit. XIII, c. 1, n. 6.

[20] C. 5, D. LXI: "Quid est cito manus imponere? Sicut enim boni operis sibi conparat fructum, qui rectum tenet in eligendo sacerdotem iudicium, ita grave semetipsum afficit damna qui ad suae dignitatis collegium sublimat indignum."

[21] Cf. the gloss of Rufinus (Summa Decretorum, [ed. H. Singer, Paderborn, 1902] D. LXVII) on a canon of the Council of Seville (619): ". . . ceteri consacerdotes et cives assensum praebeant, et eis bonum testimonium perhibeant."—Bruns, II, 70; Thomassinus, Pars II, lib. II, cap. I, n. 8; c. 119, C. I. q. 1: " . . . graves expertosque

The sources do not evince that the external vocation to the simple priesthood was ever rendered nugatory by any superior prelate for the reason simply that the advice and the testimony of others had not previously been sought and obtained by the bishop who admitted the candidate to Orders. Indeed, Thomassinus wrote that, when the presence of necessary qualities was detected in the ordinand, frequently the bishop ordained him and only afterwards informed the faithful that a new priest was given to them.[22] But in the case of the selection of a bishop, on the contrary, the testimonial consent of both the clergy and the people—their *iuramenta*—was decreed by Pope Innocent III (1198-1216) to be a prerequisite for a valid choice of one destined for the episcopacy.[23]

---

viros consilii vestri adhibete participes, et cum eis communi [de] hoc deliberatione pensate." Ioannes Teutonicus (*Glossa Ordinaria,* ad c. 8, D. LXIII, s. v. *non licet*) noted this limitation on the influence of the faithful: "... [laici] tantum debent consentire, non autem eligere, nisi hoc habeant ex privilegio speciali."

[22] Pars II, lib. II, cap. I, n. 8.

[23] C. 17, X, *de electione et electi potestate,* I, 6; Potthast, n. 836.

CHAPTER III

TRIDENTINE LEGISLATION RELATIVE TO THE ECCLESIASTICAL VOCATION

The twenty-third session of the Council of Trent restated the traditional norms governing the sacrament of Orders and enacted some new legislation, particularly concerning the constitution, officials, support and discipline of ecclesiastical seminaries. Obviously the aim of the Council's detailed and epochal treatment of these matters was the extirpation of prevalent abuses.

The widespread unobservance of canonical prescriptions for licit ordination had provided a commission composed of Cardinals and other prelates with ample material for the formulation of a series of constructive criticisms submitted in a report made to Pope Paul III (1534-1549). These findings comprised a sharp indictment of any culpable negligence in the issuance of the ecclesiastical vocation to men unqualified for the priesthood and so uncalled to it. The recommendations of this commission were preparatory to the legislation of the Council of Trent. The report given Pope Paul III pointed out that innumerable scandals, together with a detrimental effect upon religion and a lessening of the Church's spiritual prestige, resulted whenever unfit candidates were permitted to receive Orders.[1]

Some of the evils mentioned by this commission grew out of the abuses connected with secular interference in the choice of ministers. It was to remedy this that the Council enacted its decree which excluded from legitimate entry into

[1] Cf. Concilium Delectorum Cardinalium et Aliorum Prelatorum de Emendanda Ecclesia: "... passim quicumque sint, imperitissimi sint, vilissimo genere orti, sint malis moribus ornati, sint adolescentes, admittantur ad ordines sacros, et maxime ad presbyteratum, ad characterem, inquam, Christum maxime exprimentem. Hinc innumera scandala, hinc contemptus ordinis ecclesiastici, hinc divini cultus veneratio non tantum diminuta, sed etiam prope iam extincta."—Mansi, XXXV, 349.

the ministry those who were summoned to Orders by the laity or by civil authority. Those who accepted such an uncanonical call were undeserving of the title "ecclesiastical minister" and were rather likened to thieves who break in unlawfully.[2] This disavowal by the Council of any authority in the laity or the state to invite candidates to Orders was extended as well to all claims that at least subsequent to the Church's official call the consent of the faithful or of the state was required for licit ordination.[3] To exclude trespassers and those unworthy of ordination for other reasons, the Tridentine legislation enacted stringent norms controlling the examination of candidates to be conducted by bishops and by their consultors,[4] and this decree was interpreted by St. Alphonsus Liguori as a wise precaution against the giving of the ecclesiastical call to anyone not divinely invited to Holy Orders.[5]

The previously remarked trend of the Church's legislation to acknowledge the definitive selection of future priests as an episcopal prerogative was further strengthened by the Tridentine law. The conciliar Fathers made of this right not simply a matter of legislation but even a point of definite doctrine in so far as any attempt might be concerned with impugning the validity of ordinations performed without the call or at least the consent of the faithful or of the secular arm.[6] Thus the Council placed in contradistinction the true

[2] *De ordine*, c. 4: "... eos, qui tantummodo a populo, aut saeculari potestate ac magistratu vocati et instituti ad haec ministeria exercenda adscendunt, et qui ea propria temeritate sibi sumunt, omnes non ecclesiae ministros, sed fures et latrones per ostium non ingressos habendos esse."—Mansi, XXXIII, 139.

[3] Sess. XXIII, *de ordine*, c. 4: "Docet insuper sacrosancta Synodus, in ordinatione episcoporum, sacerdotum et ceterorum ordinum nec populi, nec cuiusvis saecularis potestatis et magistratus consensum, sive auctoritatem ... requiri ...."—Mansi, XXXIII, 139.

[4] Cf. sess. XXIII, *de ref.*, c. 7—Mansi, XXXIII, 142.

[5] Cf. *Theologia Moralis*, Lib. VI, n. 802.

[6] Sess. XXIII, *de ordine*, can. 7: "Si quis dixerit ... ordines ab ipsis [episcopis] collatos sine populi vel potestatis saecularis consensu aut vocatione irritos esse ... a.s."—Mansi, XXXIII, 140.

and lawful vocation—given by the Church—and the pseudo-vocation extended by anyone outside the ecclesiastical hierarchy. The wording of the decree did not exclude the advice or testimony of others concerning a candidate; it simply defined that the conferring of Orders did not prove inefficacious for the lack of the call or the consent given by the people or the secular power.

The juridical right of a bishop to determine with finality who should obtain ecclesiastical vocations in his diocese received support from the Council of Trent when it required pastors and mentors to submit to the ordinary's scrutiny precise information on the priestly qualities of their charges. This testimony had to be available to the ordinary sufficiently prior to ordination so as to allow him to rule on the canonical suitability of the prospective ordinand.[7] Again, no cleric in Minor Orders enjoyed the *privilegium fori* unless he held an ecclesiastical benefice, or, while wearing the clerical garb and tonsure, served by the bishop's command at some church, or, finally, lived at some seminary, school or university with the permission of the bishop and in preparation for the reception of Major Orders.[8] Furthermore, it was the bishop, to the exclusion of all others, upon whom was placed the responsibility for the careful and decisive investigation of the qualities of the candidate. This examination either cleared or closed the way to an ecclesiastical vocation, since it was precisely the qualities to be sought in the aspirant which constituted the prerequisites to his licit ordination.[9]

In another section of its legislation the Council determined that bishops were primarily accountable for the enforcement of those obligatory norms through the observance of which the moral and intellectual formation of clerical students was to become duly achieved. Evidence of a lack of suitability

[7] Cf. sess. XXIII, *de ref.*, c. 5—Mansi, XXXIII, 143.

[8] Sess. XXIII, *de ref.*, c. 6—Mansi, XXXIII, 143.

[9] Cf. sess. XXIII, *de ref.*, c. 7: "Episcopus . . . ordinandorum genus, personam, aetatem, institutionem, mores, doctrinam et fidem diligenter investiget et examinet."—Mansi, XXXIII, 143.

for the priestly life furnished adequate cause for prompt expulsion from the seminary, and the duty of dismissing any unworthy students rested upon the bishop, who was obliged to conduct himself most diligently in this regard. The decree setting up this obligation clearly confined final discretionary power relative to ecclesiastical vocation to the ambit of episcopal jurisdiction, granting to seminary officials no more than a consultative voice in the selection of ordinands.[10] Similarly the Council entrusted to residential bishops the exclusive faculty of deciding in every instance whether or not the necessity or the utility of their dioceses called for the ordination of any candidate.[11]

Cognate papal acts after the Council of Trent and prior to the Code uniformly established the conclusive effect of the episcopal call. At the same time these directives of the Holy See served to distinguish the concept of the divine-internal vocation from that of the ecclesiastical-external vocation by conditioning the issuance of the latter upon manifest evidence of the probable presence of the former.[12]

[10] Sess. XXIII, *de ref.*, c. 18: "Episcopi ... dyscolos et incorrigibiles, ac malorum morum seminatores acriter punient, eos etiam, si opus fuerit, expellendo, omniaque impedimenta auferentes, quaecumque ad conservandum et augendum tam pium et sanctum institutum pertinere videbuntur diligenter curabunt."—Mansi, XXXIII, 147. According to Maupied (*Juris Canonici Universi Compendium* [2 vols., Paris: Migne, 1863], Vol. I, pars III, col. 1093-1094) this episcopal prerogative was not subject to delegation.

[11] Cf. sess. XXIII, *de ref.*, c. 16: "Cum nullus debeat ordinari, qui iudicio sui episcopi non sit utilis aut necessarius suis ecclesiis ...."—Mansi, XXXIII, 146. Cf. also Innocent XIII, const. *Apostolici ministerii*, 23 maii 1723, § 3—*Fontes*, n. 280. Recourse to Rome was possible in the event of a capricious and unjustified rejection, but even in such a case the ordination was to be performed by another bishop. —Cf. S.C.C., *Asculana*, 21 apr. 1792—*Fontes*, n. 3877.

[12] Cf. Leo XIII, ep. *Iampridem*, 6 ian. 1886, n. 7: "...non aliis quam Episcopis ius munusque esse docendi et instituendi iuvenes, quos Deus singulari beneficio ex hominibus assumit, ut sint ministri sui ac dispensatores Mysteriorum suorum."—*Fontes*, n. 593; Pius IX, allocut. *Singulari quadam*, 9 dec. 1854, n. 10—*Fontes*, n. 518; Pius X, ep. *Sollicito*, 5 maii 1905—*Fontes*, n. 667. The extensive purview

CHAPTER IV

THE LAW OF THE CODE RELATIVE TO ECCLESIASTICAL VOCATION

ARTICLE 1. THE ORDINARY MINISTER OF VOCATION

A. THE BISHOP AS THE ORDINARY MINISTER

As pointed out previously, the intent of canonical legislation has regularly been to constitute (residential) bishops as the primary and principal source of external vocations to the priesthood. Since the bishop is the chief shepherd of that portion of the universal Church wherein he exercises ordinary legislative, judicial and coercive power,[1] it is accordingly to him that anyone must look for a share in the pastoral charge. The Code itself has reaffirmed this traditional discipline by allowing the bishops the full and unfettered determination of who is necessary or useful for his diocese,[2] and the bishop's judgment relative to the canonical qualities of a candidate is a prerequisite for the latter's licit ordination.[3] The basis of the ordinary's broad discretionary

---

of the bishop's power relative to the issuance or denial of the ecclesiastical vocation is aptly illustrated by his right (and obligation) of preventing a candidate's ordination even when the cause of his adverse decision is incriminating information not of itself public or certain, but sufficiently evident to the ordinary so as to warn him against acceptance of the (even occultly) unqualified aspirant. This prohibition of ascent *ex informata conscientia* is provided for by canon 970. The law of the Council of Trent as stated in sess. XIV, *de ref.*, c. 1, and authorizing this prohibition, introduced a change in the Decretal Law. By the disposition of the latter a bishop was not permitted, for whatever reason, to prohibit extra-judicially a candidate from being ordained, but was allowed simply to warn a suspected delinquent against seeking ordination.—Cf. c. 5, X, *de temporibus ordinationum et qualitate ordinandorum*, I, 11. The Tridentine decree was reiterated by Pope Benedict XIV in the constitution *Ad militantis*, 30 mart. 1742, § 23— *Fontes*, n. 326.

[1] Canons 329, § 2; 335, § 1. [2] Canon 969, § 1. [3] Canon 968, § 1.

authority in the admission to or rejection from the reception of Holy Orders is found in the very nature of the priesthood itself as instituted for the spiritual benefit of the faithful. Who, better than the bishop, can fittingly determine how the common spiritual welfare of a particular diocese may be most perfectly served?[4]

B. OTHER ORDINARY MINISTERS

The bishop has up till now been specifically mentioned as the ordinary minister of vocation with a view to emphasizing the nature of the ecclesiastical vocation as an act emanating from the Church's hierarchy of jurisdiction, wherein the residential episcopacy is the most conspicuous office. Due to the bishop's outstanding position in the hierarchy it has been thought serviceable to treat of external vocation simply as a function of the episcopal power. However, the privilege and obligation to supply priests for the Church is an exercise of that jurisdictional authority which is vested in anyone who, in virtue of his office or by concession of general law, is empowered to summon candidates to Orders. This is the signification of the text in the Catechism of the Council of Trent: ". . . they are called by God who are called by the lawful ministers of His Church."[5] Thus the ordinary ministers of vocation are, besides residential bishops, the Sovereign Pontiff;[6] vicars and prefects apostolic, abbots and prelates *nullius;*[7] vicars capitular under specified conditions;[8] vicars general when authorized with a special mandate;[9] and, finally, major superiors of exempt

[4] Cf. canon 334, § 1: "Episcopi residentiales sunt ordinarii et immediati pastores in dioecesibus sibi commissis."; canon 335, § 1: "Ius ipsis et officium est gubernandi dioecesim tum in spiritualibus tum in temporalibus . . . ." Cf. also Wernz-Vidal, *Ius Canonicum,* II, n. 573.

[5] *Catechism of The Council of Trent for Parish Priests, The Sacrament of Holy Orders,* pp. 318-319.

[6] Canon 218, § 1.

[7] Canons 294, § 1; 957, § 1; 958, § 1, 4°.

[8] Canon 958, § 1, 3°.

[9] Canon 958, § 1, 2°.

religious institutes.[10] The extent of this power—which can ultimately be reduced to the juridical capacity to issue dimissorial letters—is unlimited with respect either to the person or to territory in the case of the Supreme Pontiff; it is limited territorially in the case of a bishop, a vicar or prefect apostolic, an abbot or prelate *nullius,* a vicar capitular or a vicar general. Superiors of exempt religious institutes[11] are limited to the persons subject to them in the exercise of their jurisdictional authority, in accordance with the provisions of their proper constitutions.[12]

The ecclesiastical vocation of the members of all non-exempt religious communities is controlled by the law relating to the secular clergy,[13] and in the absence of a special privilege[14] these members receive their call to Orders from their proper bishop in keeping with the general provisions of canon 956. Therefore, the superiors of such institutes are not ordinary ministers of vocation for the professed members of their communities. Rather they must furnish to the proper bishop testimony concerning the ordinand's canonical suitability and by a recommendation the superior in effect asks the bishop to grant a vocation to the religious.[15]

ARTICLE 2. THE DELEGATED MINISTERS OF VOCATION

In addition to those who are enabled by their office to issue the ecclesiastical vocation the Code also mentions others who can share that jurisdictional power. These are such as have been commissioned to act in virtue of the principles of dele-

[10] Canon 964, 2°.

[11] Canon 964, 2°, states: "Religiosi exempti a nullo Episcopo ordinari licite possunt sine litteris dimissoriis proprii Superioris maioris." From this it would seem that the major superior of an exempt lay institute is empowered to give an ecclesiastical vocation. An instance of this kind is in evidence when a brother of the Order of St. John of God is called to the priesthood by his provincial superior.

[12] Cf. canon 501, § 1.

[13] Canon 964, 4°.

[14] *Acta Sanctae Sedis* (41 vols., Romae, 1865-1908), I (1865-1866), 366. Cf. also Wernz-Vidal, *Ius Canonicum,* IV, n. 198.

[15] Cf. canon 993, 5°.

gation and subdelegation as set forth in canon 199, even when such participated power may derive simply through an ordinary's act of tacit delegation. An ordinary's use of delegates in this matter appears certainly practical and almost imperative when one considers the difficulties of time and place, and the press of other duties confronting an ordinary. Frequently he has little or no opportunity personally to determine the fitness of each candidate.

The nexus between the question of vocation and the function of delegates is placed in relief through a correlation of canon 1353 with canons 972 and 1354, § 2. Canon 1353 places upon priests in general and pastors in particular a fourfold obligation in respect to boys who show indications of divine vocation: 1) to safeguard them against moral contagion; 2) to instruct them in piety; 3) to imbue them with learning that is proportioned to their capacity; 4) to nurture in them the vocational "seed". Canon 972 has reference to such youths when it speaks of the care to be taken that they be admitted early into the seminary, or at least be entrusted to the diligent care of an approved priest, and canon 1354, § 2 provides for the establishment of minor and major seminaries to prepare promising young men for the priesthood. Thus the seed of a vocation, placed in the soul of a youth by divine grace, is cultivated by priests who may in time become the ordinary's delegate for the final issuance of the ecclesiastical call to Orders.

The erection of seminaries according to the Tridentine legislation[16] and the law incorporated in Book III, Title XXI, of the Code is designed to satisfy and bring to fruition the fourfold duty initially incumbent upon priests and pastors as determined in canon 1353. In this way the entire matter of vocation is ineluctably joined to the law respecting the administration of clerical seminaries.

As the official primarily charged with the well-being of a designated portion of the Church,[17] a bishop's personal

[16] Cf. sess. XXIII, *de ref.*, c. 18—Mansi, XXXIII, 147.

[17] Canons 334, § 1; 335, § 1.

responsibility to discover and promote priestly vocations is specified by canon 1357, § 1, which exacts of him a strict vigilance and careful supervision over the administration and discipline of diocesan seminaries. The ambit of the episcopal obligation to assure a constant supply of priests for the needs of the faithful is outlined in the prescriptions of canon 1357, § 2.[18]

While it is evident from the conclusions adduced in the preceding article that the definitive act of selecting the ordinand depends solely upon the unimpeded decision of the ordinary who alone lawfully admits aspirants to the seminary,[19] yet in practice much that is preambulatory and directive of that final choice rests within the discretion of seminary officials, especially of the rector. The direct and daily contact of the seminary staff with students offers these officials a valuable opportunity to determine, with a high degree of accuracy, the fitness and probable vocation of an ecclesiastical student. And so the opinion of a seminary faculty regarding the canonical suitability of candidates is of notable worth to an ordinary when the time arrives for

[18] "Potissimum studeat Episcopus frequenter Seminarium ipse per se visitare, in institutionem quae alumnis traditur sive litterariam et scientificam sive ecclesiasticam sedulo vigilare, et de alumnorum indole, pietate, vocatione ac profectu pleniorem sibi comparare notitiam, maxime occasione sacrarum ordinationum." Cf. Benedict XIV, ep. encycl. *Ubi primum*, 3 dec. 1740, § 2: "Et quoniam supra quam dici possit, interest eos, qui in sortem Domini vocantur, ab ineunte aetate ad pietatem, morumque integritatem, et ad canonicam disciplinam, veluti novellas plantationes in iuventute sua, informari.... Eadem vero Collegia singulari vestra sollicitudine foveantur, necesse est, videlicet ea saepe invisendo, singulorum adolescentium vitam, indolem, et in studiis profectum explorando...."—*Fontes*, n. 304; Pius X, motu propr. *Sacrorum antistitum*, 1 sept. 1910, n. VII: "Duo igitur haec ad promovendos clericos omnino requirantur; innocentia vitae cum doctrinae sanitate coniuncta: Neve illud praetereat, praecepta ac monita, quibus episcopi sacris ordinibus initiandos compellant, non minus ad hos quam ad candidatos esse conversa, prout ubi dicitur: 'Providendum, ut caelestis sapientia, probi mores et diuturna iustitiae observatio ad id electos commendet....'"—*Fontes*, n. 689.

[19] Canon 1363, § 1.

him to decide whether or not the Church's call to Orders shall issue.[20] The Code recognizes the importance of the help given the bishop by the priests in charge of the diocesan seminary when it legislates regarding the appointment of seminary officials. These include the rector, entrusted with the over-all supervision of seminary discipline; the professors; a procurator occupied with the material concerns of the house; at least two ordinary confessors, and a spiritual director.[21] The qualities as required to be present in these authorities and listed in canon 1360, § 1, are certainly such as can guarantee an efficient and fruitful conduct of the seminary, and can assure a prudent exercise of judgment relative to the priestly vocation of the seminarians.

Although the Code does not anywhere directly require the ordinary to seek and obtain a formal vote from seminary officials concerning the advisability of admitting one to Sacred Orders, yet such an arrangement seems most consonant with the tenor of canon 1361, § 3, in so far as by this canon is expressly excluded only the mind of confessors when the question of allowing students to go on for Orders is under consideration. Effectively the same result that could be obtained by means of a formal *votum* is achieved through an observance of the disposition of the Instruction *Quam ingens,* issued by the Sacred Congregation of the Sacraments, December 27, 1930, which places upon the seminary rector a special obligation, after consultation with his staff, to inform the ordinary regarding the vocational suitability of the candidate for ordination. Since it is not to be assumed that an ordinary will often disregard such cogent testimony, the expressed opinion of seminary authorities becomes *de facto* and *de iure* almost tantamount to the ecclesiastical call to ordination.[22]

[20] Cf. Pius X, motu propr. *Sacrorum antistitum,* 1 sept. 1910, n. VII: "Videant ergo moderatores disciplinae ac pietatis, quam de se quisque spem iniiciant alumni, introspiciantque singulorum quae sit indoles . . . ."—*Fontes*, n. 689.

[21] Canon 1358.

[22] Cf. instr. *Quam ingens,* § 2, n. 5: "Quum Seminarii moderator

Besides the seminary officials the Code envisions the establishment also of two corps of advisers, consisting each of two priests. Of these bodies, one is concerned with the interior discipline of the seminary, the other with its temporal administration.[23] The Code does not indicate exactly what matters are comprised within the scope of duties of these two committees but simply requires the bishop to ask their advice in business of greater moment.[24]

An examination of the sources of canon 1359 reveals that the affairs of greater importance therein referred to are relevant to the question of ecclesiastical vocation, since they include among other matters, the admission of students to the seminary; the regulation of discipline there; the mental and moral formation of the seminarians; the punishment and dismissal of delinquents.[25] The Code neither requires nor forbids the *coetus deputatorum* to reside in the seminary when it excludes from membership the rector, the procura-

---

Episcopo remittit notitias a se collectas illius mandato, suum pandat iudicium seu opinionem suam manifestet exinde habitam de candidati moribus et ingenio. Huiusmodi iudicium non parvi ponderis profecto erit: siquidem praesumitur, moderatorem, prae ceteris, de alumnis rectum iudicium fore laturum."—*AAS*, XXIII (1931), 123.

[23] Canon 1359, § 1.

[24] Canon 1359, § 4. For a full analysis of their functions cf. Appendix XXII, *ASS*, I (1865-1866), 691. Since the *coetus deputatorum* is an institute of Tridentine legislation taken into the new law, no major changes in the constitution and work of the *coetus* have occurred. Cf. instr. *Quam ingens*, § 2, n. 5: "Quia in seminariis dioecesanis coetus adesse debet deputatorum pro disciplina tuenda ad normam can. 1359, hi etiam, si de personis edocti sint, percontandi erunt in scrutiniis faciendis."—*AAS*, XXIII (1931), 123.

[25] Cf. Conc. Trident., sess. XXIII, *de ref.*, c. 18—Mansi, XXXIII, 147; S.C.C., *Oscen.*, mense oct. 1585—*Fontes*, n. 2144; S.C.C., *Salernitana*, mense iul. 1589, § 2: "An eorum consilium adhibendum tam in constituendis regulis universalibus Seminarii ... ut puta electione singulorum puerorum introducendorum ... punitione, discolorum expulsione, visitatione, et similibus .... Ad 2: In omnibus his adhibendum."—*Fontes*, n. 2211; ep. encycl. S.C.C., 15 mart. 1897: "Nec minori claritate innotescit, in quibusnam negotiis consultorum votum sit exquirendum; in omnibus scilicet, quae tum ad disciplinam et educationem clericorum ... spectant."—*Fontes*, n. 4301.

tor and the ordinary confessors.[26] Except in those instances wherein these consultors happen to dwell among the seminarians, their awareness of a student's qualifications would of course be strictly limited to whatever information they might be able to obtain from other sources. Indeed the tenor of the directives explaining their functions indicates that their office is more properly carried out on the level of policy-making and planning than on the level of examining the probable vocation of individual aspirants.

In the case of interdiocesan or regional seminaries the Holy See itself legislates on the entire administration of such institutions,[27] either immediately through the promulgation of formal constitutive decrees,[28] or mediately through the approval of the acts of the provincial council which established the seminary in question.[29] Except for certain possible accidental details pertaining to the duties of the officials of interdiocesan or regional seminaries, the same general principles regarding the determination and cultivation of vocations will prevail in these as prevail in the diocesan seminaries.[30]

The administrators of seminaries belonging to non-exempt religious institutes—which do not regularly enjoy the power to issue dimissorial letters—are correctly considered as delegates of the candidate's proper bishop, since these communities are in this matter governed by the law respecting students destined for the secular priesthood.[31] Among Orders exempt by the common law and congregations exempt by privilege, the existence and duties of any delegated ministers of vocation must be decided from a study of their particular constitutions and customs regulating the selection of aspirants for the religious priesthood.

[26] Canon 1359, § 2.
[27] Canon 1357, § 4.
[28] Canon 1354, § 3.
[29] Cf. Beste, *Introductio in Codicem*, p. 661.
[30] Cf. *AAS*, XIV (1922), 457.
[31] Cf. canon 964, § 4.

CHAPTER V

THE JURIDICAL DOCTRINE REGARDING THE SIGNS OF VOCATION

ARTICLE 1. The Nature of the Sign of Vocation

A divine vocation to the priesthood is essentially something intangible—a grace—and accordingly its existence is incapable either of immediate scrutiny or of direct proof. Nevertheless, inasmuch as a vocation is a positive fact with profound significance in the strictly canonical order,[1] the law of the Church has never been satisfied to permit the issuance of an ecclesiastical call to Orders to be predicated on a merely gratuitous assumption that a particular individual has been divinely called to the holy priesthood.[2] Consequently the discipline governing the reception of the Sacrament of Orders has consistently required positive evidence of one's divine vocation before it has permitted ministers of ecclesiastical vocation to issue the external invitation to the priesthood. Hierarchical authority can lawfully choose one for ordination only upon the condition that it judges him called by God to the sacred ministry. This condition is postulated by the mediatory character of the priesthood.

The evidence in view of which jurisdictional power exercises its prerogative of conferring a canonical summons to Orders, consists precisely in the presence in a candidate of such qualities as are calculated to raise a solid presumption that a providential decree has destined him for the priesthood. Obviously, if an all-wise Creator chooses one for a certain office, He will at the same time endow him with the aptitude needed for the proper fulfillment of that office,

[1] Cf. Beste, *Introductio in Codicem,* p. 517.

[2] Cf. Gasparri, *De Sacra Ordinatione,* n. 110; Gregorius Magnus, *In Primum Regnum,* lib. V, c. III, n. 7—*MPL,* LXXIX, 450: "[Episcopi] qui ungunt quos non monstrat Deus."

and so the suitability of a candidate for the exigencies peculiar to the dignity and burdens of the priesthood creates a (moral) certitude that God has set him apart to serve in His ministry.

Moreover, it seems a postulate of divine wisdom that God's will respecting a matter of such grave importance for the faithful as the selection of priests, would be susceptible of discernment with sufficient accuracy to preclude all serious danger of error in the choice that needs to be made. This certitude is derived from a judgment based on the fitness of one for the priesthood, a fitness recognized as divine in origin and purpose, while remaining measurable by humanly designed standards. *Thus the various qualities of soul and body demanded in the law for the licit reception of ordination and which at the same time coalesce to evince a complete canonical worthiness for the reception of Orders, are at once constitutive and significative: constitutive of suitability and significative of the divine call which has selected and prepared the candidate for the sacred ministry.* One's total aptitude for the clerical state—the complex of talents and capacities that compose the called-for suitability —thus offers indirect but persuasive evidence of a divine vocation by serving as a sign or token of the presence of that vocation.[3] Canonical fitness does not therefore merely create ecclesiastical vocability; it is a positive sign of divine vocation.

There is no indication in canonical compilations or commentaries of any explicit recognition of the doctrine of vocational signs *qua* signs anterior to the monumental work of Hallier, published in 1633.[4] But the genesis of this legal

[3] Cf. St. Thomas Aquinas, *Summa Theologica,* Ia-IIae, q. 112, a. 5: "...cognoscitur aliquid coniecturaliter per aliqua signa." The present study is not concerned with extraordinary and miraculous signs of vocation as described, v. g., by Gregory the Great.—Cf. lib. VII, *Epis. IV—MPL,* LXXVII, 855. These transcend the ambit of canonical interest and pertain rather to a higher spiritual domain.

[4] Cf. Hallier, Pars I, sect. III, cap. II, n. 23: "Divinae vocationis quaenam sint indicia." Cf. also St. Alphonsus Liguori, *Theologia*

concept—at least in embryonic form—can be traced to the papal decrees and conciliar legislation contained in the *Corpus Iuris Canonici* and requiring in an ordinand the combination of such gifts of grace and nature as formed and betokened true suitability for the priesthood. The absence of these qualities impeded licit ordination.[5]

The perfections of soul and body that have come to be interpreted as signs or marks of an internal vocation[6] have traditionally been the very qualities to be sought for by ordinaries and their delegates in the examinations required to be conducted prior to the ecclesiastical vocation, in order that thereby the sacred ministry might be protected against entrance by such as were unfitted for it.[7]

ARTICLE 2. THE SIGNIFICATION OF THE "INDICIA" OF CANON 1353

A. CONTEXTUAL CRITICISM OF THE CANON

The Code admits the existence and cognoscibility of criteria for determining in individual instances whether one has a probable vocation to the priesthood. This it does when it exhorts priests to seek out boys who evince the marks of

Moralis, Lib. VI, n. 803; Van Espen, *Jus Ecclesiasticum Universum*, Vol. III, tit. 5, cap. 1, n. 13: "... soli ii vocari censentur, qui in se tam internae, quam externae vocationis sufficientia indicia habent."

[5] The *capable* subject of sacred ordination is any baptized male who, if an adult, intends to receive the sacerdotal character. By divine law no other conditions are requisite for the *validity* of Orders. Cf. c. 52, C. I, q. 1—I General Council of Nicaea (325), c. 19—Hefele, I, 616; c. 19, D. XXXII—Council of Laodicea (343/381), c. 11—*MPG*, XLII, 739.

[6] Cf. canon 1353: "... qui indicia praebeant ecclesiasticae vocationis ...."; Gasparri, *De Sacra Ordinatione*, n. 659; Many, *Praelectiones de Sacra Ordinatione*, p. 211; Regatillo, *Ius Sacramentarium*, II, n. 74; Coronata, *De Sacramentis*, II, n. 49.

[7] Cf. c. 34, X, *de electione et electi potestate*, I, 6; Potthast, n. 1653; c. 5, D. XXIV; Mansi, XVIII, 169; c. 2, D. XXIV—III Council of Carthage (397), c. 22—Mansi, III, 867; c. 3, D. LXXVIII; Jaffé, n. 410; c. 117, C. I, q. 1; Jaffé, n. 1379; and c. 119, C. I, q. 1; Jaffé, n. 1253.

a vocation, and encourages them to nurture in likely youths the seed of that vocation.[8] While canon 1353 does not state in so many words that these marks are signs which warrant the inference that God has destined their subject for the reception of Orders, still such an understanding of it is assuredly warranted both by the text and the context of the canon as collated with papal pronouncements pertaining to this question. Furthermore, this interpretation seems indicated in the light of the treatment hitherto presented, that is, in consequence of the very nature of the priestly calling as intended for the spiritual benefit of the visible Church. For if a vocation is something divine; if it is a special and God-given grace, then certainly there must be notes by which ecclesiastical authority might be enabled reasonably to conjecture that God's will has antecedently elected and prepared this or that young man for the ministry.

Not all authors accept this line of argumentation, either for the reason that they do not regard a candidate's suitable qualities as signs of vocation or indications of God's will,[9] or similarly, they believe simply that a vocation consists in suitability. According to this view the action of God's will in relation to vocation is consequent upon the ecclesiastical call, not antecedent to it. When the Church gives its summons to ordination, God, in effect, ratifies that choice. Therefore it follows that signs *qua* signs are fictional, and the concept of antecedent divine vocation is destitute of any reality in the concrete order.[10]

[8] Canon 1353. Cf. Leo XIII, ep. encycl. *Depuis le jour,* 8 sept. 1899, n. 9: "Il faut que leur attention [des prêtres], leur zèle, leur dévouement soient sans cesse en éveil et en action, d'une part pour étudier continuellement sous le regard et dans la lumière de Dieu, les âmes des enfants et les indices significatifs de leur vocation au service des autels. . . ."—*Fontes,* n. 642.

[9] Cf. Blowick, *Priestly Vocation,* p. 181.

[10] Cf. Vermeersch, *Epitome Iuris Canonici,* II, 242: "Voluntate Dei *consequente* ipsam externam assumptionem, vocantur quotquot rite assumpti sunt ab Ecclesia, cui delectus sacerdotum commissa est . . . His autem notis *idoneitatis* et *rectae intentionis* vera vocatio componitur." (Italics are Vermeersch's.)

An opinion that denies any juridical value to the extant marks of a vocation, or disclaims the existence of a real distinction between the signs of a vocation and the vocation itself, attempts thereby to vitiate the force of the phrase *"qui indicia praebeant ecclesiasticae vocationis"* of canon 1353. The logical consequence of this denial or disclaimer is the rejection of the entity signified by "... *divinaeque in eis vocationis germen foveant"* of the same canon. If the divine call to Orders is, in the final analysis, identifiable with fitness for the priesthood, then *ipso facto* there is excluded the notion of divine vocation as adding anything to the character of suitability. And if this exclusion be admitted then the legislator has introduced into canon 1353 some entirely superfluous words. If this unlikely hypothesis of superfluous phraseology be in turn accepted, then evidently an amended diction of canon 1353 would more logically (and succinctly) exhort priests to search for youths *"qui idoneitatem ad ordines praebeant."* Such is not the import of this canon.

It is of interest as well as of assistance in connection with this issue to note that canon 538, in referring to admission to the religious state, employs the word *"idoneus"* in defining who may lawfully enter the religious life.[11] And yet the

[11] "In religionem admitti potest quilibet catholicus qui nullo legitimo detineatur impedimento rectaque intentione moveatur, et ad religionis onera ferenda sit idoneus." The word *"idoneus"* seems to have here the sense either of suitability for the religious state in general or for some specific institute in particular. Thus Bouscaren-Ellis (*Canon Law—A Text and Commentary* [Bruce: Milwaukee, 1946], p. 258) applied the word in the general sense of mental, moral and physical qualities necessary to bear the burdens and to fulfill the offices of the religious state. Blat (*Commentarium Textus Codicis Iuris Canonici,* Lib. II, Pars II-III [3. ed., Romae, 1938], n. 282) expressly understood the requirement contained in *"idoneus"* as applicable to the religious life in general *or* to some determined community: *"Legislator igitur praemittens normam generalem, utrumque debuit respicere, quidquam nempe omnibus religionibus commune sine diversitate ipsarum et aliud peculiare uniuscuiusque religionis modo generali expressum."* Toso, on the contrary, appears to have restricted the application of *"idoneus"* to the narrower sense of suit-

schema of this canon, in contrast to its definitive form, was constructed in this wise:

> In religionem admitti potest quilibet catholicus qui nullo legitimo detineatur impedimento ac divina vocatione rectaque intentione moveatur.[12]

That the words *"divina vocatione"* were subsequently deleted in the restatement of this canon seems to indicate an intention on the part of the legislator to reserve the concept of divine vocation specifically and exclusively for the priesthood.[13] Such a studied reservation would markedly lessen the already negligible likelihood of a superfluous insertion of the phrases referring to divine vocation in canon 1353.

An insistence upon the importance of detecting in a youth the signs of vocation mentioned in canon 1353 is readily apparent in several directives issuing from Rome. These acts have accorded legal recognition to the doctrine holding that the presence of the marks is truly the sign of a divine call and really distinct from it. Thus almost contemporane-

---

ability for the work of the particular institute in question.—Cf. *Ad Codicem Juris Canonici Commentaria Minora* (5 vols., Vol. I, 2. ed. 1921; Vols. II-V, 1922-1927, Romae: Marietti), V, 87.

[12] *Schema Codicis Iuris Canonici* (ed. cum notis Petri Card. Gasparri, Romae, 1912), canon 412.

[13] Without entering here into the controversy whether or not there is truly a special divine vocation to the religious state, the writer takes occasion to express his adherence to the negative opinion. The counsels of perfection are in and of themselves *(per se)* proposed to all in general and the acceptance or the rejection of the invitation contained in the Gospel (Matt. XIX, 29) is independent of any special predetermining divine decree such as is realized in the vocation to the priesthood. Hardly any more convincing evidence in support of this position can be found than the historical fact that even infants could lawfully be offered for the religious state, but never for Sacred Orders. Cf. Benedict XIV, instr. *Eo quamvis tempore,* 4 maii 1745—*Fontes,* n. 357; Thomassinus, Lib. I, Pars II, cap. XXV, n. 3. The religious state and the priestly office are specifically distinct: the former is primarily for the sanctification of self; the latter is primarily for the sanctification of others. The Church's call alone suffices for a licit entry into the religious life, but a strictly divine vocation, in addition to the ecclesiastical call, is needed for a lawful ordination to the priesthood.

ously with the promulgation of the Code, Benedict XV described suitability for the priesthood as conditioned on indications of a divine vocation: *"Quod si pressius definiri a Nobis cupitis quos reapse habeatis idoneos, eos dicimus in quibus divinae vocationis argumenta reperietis."*[14]

A private recommendation emanating from the Sacred Congregation for Seminaries and Universities on January 24, 1928, and addressed to all the ordinaries of the United States by the Apostolic Delegate, made reference to the need of guiding boys who "manifest signs of a priestly vocation."[15] The Instruction *Quam ingens* of 1930 likewise adverted to some determined signs of vocation to be investigated by the seminary rector,[16] and a similar directive of the following year, *Quantum Religiones,* no less explicitly demanded that special signs proper to the clerical office be sought in students destined for the sacred priesthood in religious communities.[17]

In the memorable encyclical *Ad catholici sacerdotii fastigium,* Pius XI named right intention in approaching Orders; inclination to the priestly functions; spiritual, mental and physical talents; zeal; piety and purity as qualities enabling superiors to judge the authenticity of their subjects' vocation.[18]

B. CORRELATION WITH CANON 973

A correlation of canon 1353 with canon 973, §§ 1, 3, aids substantially in interpreting the concept of the *"indicia"*

[14] Ep. encycl. *Humani generis,* 15 iunii 1917—*AAS,* IX (1917), 308.

[15] The text is given in its entirety in Bouscaren, *The Canon Law Digest* (2 vols., Milwaukee: Bruce, 1934-1943), I, 647-655.

[16] § 2: "Seminarii moderator... audiet... de singularibus nempe vocationis signis, uti sunt pietas, modestia, castitas, de propensione ad sacras functiones...."—*AAS,* XXIII (1931), 123.

[17] S.C. de Religiosis, instr. *Quantum Religiones,* § 6: "... requiruntur [in candidatis ad sacerdotium designandis] praeterea signa specialia clericorum statui propria."—*AAS,* XXIV (1932), 76.

[18] III: "... is profecto, ut perspicuo patet, ad sacerdotale ministerium a Deo vocatur."—*AAS,* XXVIII (1936), 40.

which receive mention in the former canon. Canon 973, § 1, precludes even the conferment of tonsure except when there is a solid basis for the inference that a candidate will, in due time, prove to be a worthy priest.[19] But how is this conjecture of future worthiness to be formed except through a disclosure of such present qualities as manifest a radical fitness for the sacerdotal office? The apparent suitability (or unsuitability) of a student provides a frame of reference according to which ecclesiastical authority can derive a sound conclusion of the presence (or absence) of a divine vocation.

The nexus between § 1 and § 3 of canon 973 consists in this, that both paragraphs require some definite assurance of the reality of one's vocation before any promotion in clerical grades may take place, but § 3 is more stringent in its demand that a bishop have moral certitude, founded on positive arguments, of an ordinand's canonical worthiness for Holy Orders, while § 1 is satisfied to exact a reasonable conjecture of fitness for tonsure or Minor Orders. As one draws nearer the irrevocable dignity of Major Orders, and especially the priesthood, the evidence of his divine call must be proportionately more certain.[20]

When his superiors perceive that a subject possesses a complete canonical suitability for the priesthood, it can then be duly inferred that he is divinely called in the sense of canon 1353. As from the inherent configuration of some work of art one is able to determine with a high degree of accuracy the purpose for which the artisan has designed it, so also it can be prudently concluded that God has called one to His ministry whom He has equipped for it.[21]

[19] "Prima tonsura et ordines illis tantum conferendi sunt . . . quos merito coniicere liceat aliquando dignos futuros esse presbyteros."

[20] Pope Benedict XV used "*argumenta*," the same word that is used in canon 973, in the encyclical *Humani generis:* ". . . divinae vocationis argumenta . . . ."—*AAS*, IX (1917), 308. Cf. Pius IX, ep. encycl. *Cum nuper,* 20 ian. 1858, § 2—*Fontes*, n. 523.

[21] Many, *Praelectiones de Sacra Ordinatione*, p. 211. Cf. Leo XIII, ep. encycl. *Fin dal principio*, 8 dec. 1902, § 5: "Si rimandino quanti

In respect to the judgment made of an aspirant's vocation to Orders, the Code in canon 973 does not require anything more than moral certitude, but it likewise is not satisfied with anything less. This degree of certitude has the technical sense of a conviction founded on serious and weighty reasons. It is not essential that there be precluded at the same time all possibility for the truth to rest elsewhere.[22] It is the certainty a prudent man seeks before reaching his decision in a matter of serious and proportionate gravity. It is a certitude considerably more reassuring than a mere surmise or guess. Rather it is equivalent to a firm opinion, and while transcending the assurance of suspicion, it is obviously without the conviction which characterizes faith.[23]

In the actual day-to-day application of the norms laid down for the discernment of vocation there is no place for any excessively rigid interpretation of the legislator's intention in the matter of signs.[24] The appraisal of the candidate's total canonical aptitude for the priesthood is not formulated mathematically, for law itself is not a mathematical process, and the use of the doctrine of signs is an applica-

---

nel corso della loro educazione manifestassero tendenze men convenevoli alla vocazione sacerdotale, e nell' ammettere i chierici agli ordini sacri si usi somma ponderazione, giusta l'ammonimento gravissimo di San Paolo a Timoteo: *Manus cito nemini imposueris* (I Tim. V, 22)."—*Fontes*, n. 650.

[22] Cf. Nilles, *Commentarius de Vocatione ad Statum Ecclesiasticum* (Oeniponte: Pustet, 1892), p. 62: "... probabilia vocationis signa esse indicia, quae bono et aequo viro adeo fundatam opinionem divinae locutionis injiciant, ut, deficiente licet indubitata certaque veritatis fide, eam tamen minime contemnendam judicet, praesertim si plura signa coacerventur, quae variis argumentorum adminiculis invicem confirmentur."

[23] Cf. St. Thomas Aquinas, *Summa Theologica*, IIa-IIae, q. 2, a. 1: "... sive in unam partem magis declinent [actus intellectus], sed tenentur aliquo levi signo, sicut accidit suspicanti; sive uni parti adhaereant, tamen cum formidine alterius, quod accidit opinanti. Sed actus iste qui est credere, habet firmam adhaesionem ad unam partem ...."

[24] Cf. Wernz-Vidal, *Ius Canonicum*, IV, n. 216.

tion of a legal principle. It is the office of the authorities charged with the responsibility of extending the external call to evaluate carefully *all* the evidence at their disposal in order to obtain the moral certitude specified in canon 973. Thus a doubt about the full verification of some aspect of fitness might well be compensated for by strong evidence of aptitude on some other point. The entire emphasis on certitude is intended to obviate, as nearly as possible, the danger of admitting the uncalled to sacred ordination. *It should be carefully noted that it never suffices merely that nothing unfavorable is known concerning a candidate's fitness; positive evidence of his canonical suitability is always demanded.*[25]

ARTICLE 3. THE PARTICULAR SIGNS OF VOCATION

A. HISTORICAL SYNOPSIS OF THE LAW RELATIVE TO THE PARTICULAR SIGNS OF VOCATION

1. *The Basic Indispensability of Moral, Mental and Physical Suitability*

The spiritual, mental and corporal perfections required for the lawful acceptance of the priesthood are postulated primarily by the natural law. Our reason itself readily declares that anyone who enjoys the exalted dignity annexed to the conducting of divine worship and the administration of the sacraments, ought to have a character consonant with his lofty office together with becoming intellectual and physical endowments. These talents, for the most part congenital, are called for also in positive divine law.[26] Such perfections are intrinsic to the person; they are essentially

[25] Cf. Pius XI, ep. encycl. *Ad catholici sacerdotii fastigium, AAS* XXVIII (1936), 43.

[26] Cf. Leviticus, XXI, 16-21. Decretal Law used the Pauline texts of I Tim. III, 2-6, and of Titus, I, 2-9, as the frame of its legislation relative to such qualities.

independent of every human agency in the order of causality; they evidently derive from the act of Providence which prepares those who are chosen by divine decree for the priesthood. The same God Who "predestines" certain men to serve the altar also bestows upon them whatever qualities are demanded for the proper discharge of the sacred ministry. Suitability is truly a consequence of vocation.[27]

The fitness produced by these perfections is so indispensable that the ordaining of one who is notably wanting in this radical aptitude is unlawful. As Gasparri has observed, the Church's constant unwillingness to claim for itself any right to dispense from a marked deficiency in one's qualifications for the priesthood is itself evidence of the Church's disavowal of any such competence.[28]

2. *Suitability in Decretal and Tridentine Legislation*

The rather comprehensive treatment in the *Corpus Iuris Canonici* of such defects as constituted a bar to licit ordination—in later legal development many of these defects came to be classified as irregularities—[29]indicates legislation largely *praeter legem divinam.* Positive ecclesiastical law never confines itself to the incorporation merely of such prohibitions as are expressed in the divine law, but elaborates and extends the implications of that law.[30]

The numerous impediments to licit ordination based on

[27] Cf. Thomassinus, Pars II, lib. I, cap. XXVI, n. 3: "... de majoribus [ordinibus] ... divina quadam fieri sorte et providentia"; *ibid.*, cap. XXIV, n. 11: "Dei autem judicio relinquendum est, quem velit, et si velit assumere sibi ad ministerium, vel ad sacerdotium. Non enim, qui se ipsum ingesserit, sed quem Dominus assumpserit, ille probatus est."

[28] *De Sacra Ordinatione*, n. 116.

[29] There is in the *Corpus Iuris Canonici* no rubric which is *ex professo* devoted to irregularities. Their treatment falls within divers sections of Books I and V of the Decretals of Gregory IX.

[30] Cf. Wernz-Vidal, *Ius Canonicum*, IV, n. 239.

physical incapacities[31] and mental deficiencies,[32] implicitly recognized bodily soundness and intellectual acumen as signs of vocation. The prohibitory restrictions as obtaining in the case of specifically characterized impediments would *a fortiori* have impeded licit ordination when more general corporal or mental imperfection was in question. It remained within the ordinary's competence as a juridically acknowledged interpreter of the divine law to decide whether one's physical and intellectual gifts indicated a divine calling, even if no positive ecclesiastical legislation could in fact be referred to a particular case.[33]

[31] Cf. c. 1, D. LV; Jaffé, n. 636: "*corpore vitiati*"; c. 3, D. XXXIII; Jaffé, *Spuria*, n. LIII: "*epileptici*"; c. 13, D. LV; Jaffé, n. 993: "*erutus oculus*"; c. 5, D. XXXIII; Jaffé, n. 636: "*surdus et mutus*". The law as constructed in c. 2, X, *de corpore vitiatis ordinandis vel non*, I, 20 (Jaffé, n. 12367) excluded those who were too small of stature, those who were notably deformed, and those whose sex remained undeterminable. In respect to bodily defects in general which constituted a hindrance to the reception of Orders, the canonical legislation became crystallized by the time of the Decretals of Gregory IX. Subsequently this well-determined law was applied by way of interpretation or dispensation to individual cases.—Cf. Wernz-Vidal, *Ius Canonicum*, IV, n. 239.

[32] Decretal Law considered more particularly the knowledge of a candidate for Orders rather than his native intellectual abilities, but evidently knowledge was regularly proportioned to intelligence although not identified with it. Accordingly, ignorance was a bar to the licit admission into the clerical state.—Cf. c. 1, D. XXXVIII: "Ignorantia mater cunctorum errorum maxime in sacerdotibus Dei vitanda est."—Mansi, X, 626. The *Glossa Ordinaria* (ad c. 1, D. XXXVI, s.v. *oportet—illitteratos*) observed in what sense ignorance is inimical to the priesthood, but qualified the observation by adding "*sufficit tamen mediocris scientia ... non enim requiritur in clerico summa perfectio.*" Cf. Raymundus de Pennafort, *Summa* (Veronae, 1744), III, tit. 5: "... oportet et ordinandum esse prudentem: debet enim habere triplicem peritiam, videlicet sacrae scripturae ... secularium litterarum ... secularium negotiorum notitiam."

[33] Cf. c. 5, D. XXIV (Spurious)—Council of Nantes (895): "Ne indignum et minus idoneum ad sacros gradus suscipiendos episcopi manibus applicent."—Mansi, XVIII, 165. Regarding the general power of the bishop in determining the acceptability of the aspirant, cf. Thomassinus, Pars II, lib. I, cap. XXIII, *passim*.

The probity of a candidate's character was understood by Decretal Law as a condition for licit ordination, as Gregory the Great had cautioned in a letter addressed to Bishop Adeodatus in 593.[34] The primary intent of the legislator in excluding from ordination those who were recognized as morally unfit was in order that the ministry might be duly safeguarded from the dishonor associated with a life that had been one of ill repute.[35]

Thus the I General Council of Nicaea (325) excluded from ordination those who after baptism had fallen into serious sin, especially if the defection implied a carnal offense, provided that the lapse could be legally proved by at least two witnesses.[36] Even when someone had performed a public penance that freed him from the stigma of his sin, Pope Siricius (384-398) decreed the penitent still to be unworthy for Orders, since any person who had been a "vessel of vice" was not to be considered worthy to handle the sacred vessels used in the administration of the sacraments.[37] It was to prevent morally unqualified aspirants from advancing to Orders that led Pope St. Gelasius I (492-496) to require a diligent scrutiny of an ordinand's previous life, and a serious blemish in character was understood as indicative of faulty intention in seeking admission to the clerical state.[38]

Among the offenses which the *Corpus Iuris Canonici* ex-

[34] "Estote ergo praecipue in ordinatione solliciti, et ad sacros ordines nisi ... mundos opere nullatenus admittatis. Eorum, enim, qui in sacro ordine sunt collocandi, prius vitam moresque discutite."—C. 119, C. I, q. 1; Jaffé, n. 1253.

[35] Cf. Reg. 87, R.J., in VI°: "Infamibus portae non pateant dignitatum."

[36] Hefele, I, 532.

[37] C. 66, D. L; Jaffé, n. 255.

[38] C. 1, D. LV; Jaffé, n. 636: "... anteacta eius vita requiratur, ne sit aliquo facinore infectus ...." The *Glossa Ordinaria* regarded a morally offensive previous life as evidence of an improper intention: "Hic mala vita probat aliquem ambitione pervenisse ad dignitatem; sic e contrario merita alicuius excusavit ipsum de ambitione."—Ad c. 5, D. LXI, s.v. *documenta.*

plicitly designated as constituting prohibitions to the legitimate reception of Orders were fornication,[39] theft,[40] the giving of false testimony,[41] and apostasy.[42] One known to be guilty of these and similar sins was reckoned as wanting in the probity marking worthiness for the sacred ministry, and accordingly he was presumed to lack a divine calling, particularly when the transgressions were flagrant. But it should not be imagined that Decretal legislation *a priori* precluded from ordination every sinner—such an interpretation finds no warrant in the sources.[43]

Lest the esteem owed to the sacerdotal office be placed in jeopardy through the admission of one who was notoriously unworthy of it, particular effort was made to exclude those who were known to be guilty of public offenses.[44] But going beyond the implications of public infamy, the law, by insisting on proof of positive virtue, evinced a parallel solicitude to restrain from Orders those whose known deficiencies of character suggested possible future defections.[45] Even if no question of public guilt presented itself, nevertheless the subject of sacred ordination was urged personally to be convinced that his moral rectitude fitted him for the priest-

[39] C. 1, D. XXVIII; Jaffé, n. 1112: "... nullus debet ad ministerium altaris accedere, nisi cuius castitas ante susceptum ministerium fuerit approbata." The special emphasis placed upon moral purity appeared in c. 5, D. LXI; Jaffé, n. 410; c. 5, D. LI; Mansi, X, 625; c. 7, X, *de electione et electi potestate*, I, 6—III General Council of the Lateran (1179), c. 3—Mansi, XXII, 261.

[40] C. 1, D. LXXXI; *MPL*, XXV, 1697.

[41] C. 7, D. L; Mansi, VIII, 561.

[42] C. 69, D. L; Bruns, II, 133.

[43] Cf. Raymundus de Pennafort, *Summa*, III, tit. 2: "Ut ordinandus sit sine crimine, hoc non est intelligendum de quolibet crimine; quia nemo sine crimine vivit."

[44] Cf. c. 4, X, *de temporibus ordinationum et qualitate ordinandorum*, I, 12; Jaffé, n. 11527.

[45] Cf. *Glossa Ordinaria*, ad c. 119, C. I, q. 1, s.v. *estote:* "... [ordinandi] qui sunt moribus commendati ...."; Raymundus de Pennafort, *Summa*, III, tit. 7: "... debet enim ordinandus esse ornatus in virtutibus."

hood.[46] Among the virtues singled out as indicating worthiness for the clerical state were sobriety,[47] charity towards the poor,[48] equanimity,[49] and humility.[50]

By the time of the Council of Trent the law regulating the basic notions of moral, mental and physical suitability had become well settled juridical doctrine. The Council treated in a summary fashion the qualities necessary for an ordinand, but it did so in such a way as to preserve the essential demands of the prior legislation while allowing for the subsequent evolution of the notion of specific signs of a divine vocation.[51]

3. *The Right Intention*

Of salient importance in the matter of the signs of a divine vocation is the intention with which a candidate seeks ordination.[52] The Church's law has ever cautioned ecclesiastical superiors to refuse Orders to one who has shown in any way that his reason for advancing to the priesthood consisted in some motive other than in the sincere desire of promoting God's glory and saving souls through the exercise of the sacred ministry: *sacerdos propter alios*.[53]

[46] Cf. *Glossa Ordinaria,* ad c. 115, C. I, q. 1, s.v. *vocatus:* "Et etiam licet valde dignus sit, non tamen effraenata temeritate, sed trepida deliberatione onus sacerdotii debet subire"; Isidore of Seville († 636), *Sententiarum Libri,* Lib. III, c. 34: "... humiliter ad id quod vocatur accedat."—*MPL,* LXXXIII, 706.

[47] D. XLIV. [48] D. XLII. [49] D. XLIII. [50] D. XLVI.

[51] Cf. sess. XXIII, *de ref.,* c. 4, 5, 7, 11, 12, 18—Mansi, XXXIII, 142-146.

[52] "Right intention" has no direct affinity with the "intention of being ordained" which is needed for the validity itself of the conferred Orders. With its presence assumed in a baptized adult male, no degree of depravity in his motives for wishing to be ordained would render the reception of the Orders invalid. Cf. Wernz-Vidal, *Ius Canonicum,* IV, n. 207.

[53] Cf. St. Alphonsus Liguori, *Theologia Moralis,* lib. VI, n. 802: "... desiderium vacandi divinae gloriae et saluti animarum"; Thomassinus, Pars II, lib. I, cap. XXIII, n. 14: "... spiritualium et coelestium bonorum charitate [in exsequendo ordines]."

An inspection of conciliar and papal legislation directed against simony[54] and abuses related to lay investiture serves to place in relief the legislator's solicitous desire to exclude from ordination those candidates who lacked a right intention. Among papal acts bearing immediately on the evil of simony and on the consequent presumption of non-vocation was that of Pope Symmachus (498-514), wherein the Pontiff referred to the grace of God as the moving force underlying the reception of Orders with a right intention. When simony was involved that grace was considered not present.[55]

Similarly, the II General Council of Nicaea (787) in its enactments against simoniacal clerics contrasted those who had become ordained because they had paid money with those who had received Orders in accordance with the dispositions of divine Providence. The former were considered as guilty of serious fault, while the latter obtained ordination because they were elected and constituted by the Holy Spirit on account of the virtue of their lives, and not in consequence of an exchange of gold.[56] The simoniacally ordained were thus held to be without a vocation because they had entered the sacerdotal office without a divine call and a lawful summons from the Church. The licitly ordained, on the other hand, received the priestly character not only in consequence of an antecedent divine invitation but also in pursuance of a legitimate call from the Church.

Gregory VII (1073-1085), whose reforms accomplished a stricter adherence to canonical norms respecting the traditional discipline of the Sacrament of Holy Orders, inveighed against purchased ordinations as false inasmuch as they lacked the necessary juridical basis not only of the internal

[54] Gratian's *Decretum* devoted thirty *capitula* to the consideration of simony and the *Libri Decretalium* of Gregory IX yielded only a few less.

[55] Epistola *Hortatur nos:* "Illud magnopere commonens, ut hi qui non Dei gratia sed promissione rerum ecclesiasticarum praemissa ad sacerdotium conantur accedere, desideriorum talium priventur effectu."—*MPL,* LXXXIV, 811.

[56] Mansi, XIII, 425.

divine vocation, but also of the external ecclesiastical summons. One who foisted himself upon the sacred ministry through the payment of money was held not to have the intention of working for the salvation of Christ's sheep, but rather to have entered as a thief or a robber.[57]

Closely allied to the crime of simony and of nearly equal detriment to the proper concept of vocation and its essential right intention were the evils connected with lay investiture. The unflagging attempts of ecclesiastical law to eliminate these corruptive abuses were strongly indicative of the Church's solicitude to preserve intact the requirement of right intention for a licit reception of the Sacrament of Orders.[58] Subsequent conciliar and pontifical acts simply reiterated the interdictions against simony and related abuses as noted in the *Corpus Iuris Canonici,* and thereby strengthened the canonical demand for propriety of motive in the one seeking ordination.[59]

[57] C. 113, C. 1, q. 1; Jaffé, n. 5064: "Ordinationes, quae interveniente pretio ... fiunt, ... falsas esse diiudicamus, quoniam qui taliter ordinantur non per ostium, id est per Christum, intrant, sed, ut ipsa veritas testatur, fures sunt et latrones." Cf. *Glossa Ordinaria,* ad c. 113, C. 1, q. 1, s.v. *ordinationes:* "... ordinatus pretio, precibus, vel obsequio, canonice non eligitur, quia taliter ordinatus non intrat per ostium, sed fur est et latro."; c. 9, 39, X, *de simonia, et ne aliquid pro spiritualibus exigatur vel promittatur, V. 3.*

[58] Pope Lucius III (1181-1185) decreed that even when a superior had learned of the lack of right intention through *secreta commissa* the candidate was not to be admitted to ordination.—Cf. c. 4, X, *de temporibus ordinationum et qualitate ordinandorum,* I, 11; Jaffé, n. 7152. Cf. the letter of Gregory VII (1073-1085) to Hugh of Cluny (1024-1109)—*MPL,* CXLVII, 400; Thomassinus, Pars II, lib. I, cap. XXV, n. 8: "Explodendi protinus sunt, quos terrena cupiditas, non divina vocatio, clero inseruit."

[59] Cf. Conc. Trid., sess. XXI, de ref., c. 1: "Quoniam ab ecclesiastico ordine omnis avaritiae suspicio abesse debet, nihil pro collocatione quorumcumque ordinum ... episcopi et alii ordinum collatores aut eorum ministri quovis praetextu accipiant."—Mansi, XXXIII, 124; Sixtus V, const. *Sanctum et salutare,* 5 ian. 1589, § 1: "Cum enim multi etiam interdum inhabiles, et indigni, non vocati sancta Dei vocatione, sed potius Satanae dolis decepti ... temporale aliquod commodum, aut lucrum sibi proponentes ... temere se ingerant."—

B. CANONICAL COMMENTARY RELATIVE TO THE PARTICULAR SIGNS OF VOCATION

The historical treatment of the particular signs of vocation at once leads to a consideration of the role accorded them in contemporary legislation. Regarding the fundamental notions of moral, mental and physical suitability, the Code does not amplify the clearly delineated requisites of the earlier law, but in its canons the present law summarily sets forth such principles as have traditionally been accepted both in theory and in practice. The Code simply perpetuates the Church's insistence on the need for evidence of a divine vocation as furnished by the presence of specified qualifications in the subject of sacred ordination.[60]

1. *Moral Suitability*

a) Moral Fitness in General

The sign of a vocation as connoted through a moral suitability appears in several places in the Code, but necessarily in generic form. Thus canon 974, § 1, 2°, stipulates as a condition for licit ordination *"mores ordini recipiendo congruentes"*, and canon 1000, § 1, instructs the ordinary to obtain from a candidate's pastor, and even from others, written testimony pertaining to the ordinand's moral life.[61] Specific implementation of the broad requirement of canon 1000, § 1, is contained in the Instruction *Quam ingens,* particularly in the Appendix, Mod. II. The questions therein proposed and to be answered by an aspirant's pastor are of varying importance as determinants of the probable existence of a vocation. An unfavorable response to certain

Fontes, n. 166; Clement XIV, ep. encycl. *Decet quam maxime,* 21 sept. 1769, § 1: "Decet quam maxime Ecclesiae ministros, et dispensatores mysteriorum Dei, ut ab omni avaritiae suspicione, etsi levissima, penitus alieni, sacro ita vacent ministerio, ad quod vocati a Deo sunt . . . ." —*Fontes,* n. 467.

[60] Cf. Pius XI, ep. encycl. *Ad catholici sacerdotii fastigium,* 20 dec. 1935, *AAS,* XXVIII (1936), 40.

[61] Cf. also canon 993, 3°.

of the questions would produce a strong presumption of a non-vocation,[62] and the accumulative effect of this investigation, considered in conjunction with the questions set forth in Mod. III of the instruction,[63] presents incisive delineation of a candidate's moral character and thereby serves superiors in their formation of a judgment of the probable vocation.

The rule of canon 1371 which provides for the dismissal of students who prove morally unfitted for the clerical state,[64] as well as the corresponding obligation placed upon bishops to ascertain the reasons for the expulsion of a seminarian before accepting him for entrance into another seminary,[65] are enacted in view of the fundamental clerical obligation to cultivate holiness. As stated in canon 124, this obligation is applicable, by extension, to seminarians as future priests.[66]

[62] V.g.: "5. Num studium curamque prodat divinum provehendi cultum, animarum curandi bonum, atque ad sacra exercenda ministeria propensionem patefaciat; 9. Num praedictis feriis cum aliquibus utriusque sexus personis non bonae famae ... familiaritatem foverit, vel loca frequentaverit haud suspicione carentia ... ; 13. Num se proclivem exhibeat ad vitae commoda, ad copiosum hauriendum vinum, ad liquores sumendos, atque ad profana oblectamenta capienda; 15. Quae sit publica de ipsius vocatione opinio; 17. Num parentes, vel alter e familia ipsum impellant ad sacerdotium ineundum."—*AAS*, XXIII (1931), 128-129.

[63] "1. An clericus sive in ecclesia, sive in consuetudine cum aliis habenda, pie, graviter, prudenterque se gesserit ac gerat; 2. An aliquod de sua vocatione ad sacros Ordines foveri possit dubium, et qua ratione; 3. An parentes vel alter e familia ad eosdem suscipiendos sacros Ordines ipsum impellant; 4. An familiariter utatur cum iis, qui in suspicionem veniant de fidei carentia, vel de malis moribus; 5. Quae sit publica et praecipue praestantiorum hominum existimatio de agendi ratione, tum morali tum religiosa, eiusdem clerici, et de eius vocatione ad sacerdotium ineundum."—*AAS*, XXIII (1931), 129.

[64] "E Seminario dimittantur dyscoli, incorrigibiles, seditiosi, ii qui ob mores atque indolem ad statum ecclesiasticum idonei non videantur ...."

[65] Canon 1363, § 3.

[66] Cf. Pius XI, ep. encycl. *Ad catholici sacerdotii fastigium,* 20 dec. 1935, *AAS,* XXVIII (1936), 23; Gibbons, *The Ambassador of Christ*

The discipline relating to ill repute (*infamia*), whether it be such in fact[67] or in law,[68] is linked to the problem of vocation in so far as ill repute or infamy furnishes a presumption against moral aptitude. Its evidential value in relation to vocation must be assayed according to the circumstances surrounding individual cases. The cessation of infamy in fact, effected in accordance with canon 2295 through the prudent judgment of the ordinary, particularly when an earnest amendment is indeed manifest, may lessen the presumption of non-vocation. But, when one considers the very definition of infamy in fact:

> Infamia facti contrahitur, quando quis, ob patratum delictum vel ob pravos mores, bonam existimationem apud fideles probos et graves amisit, de quo iudicium spectat ad Ordinarium.[69]

it seems that such a presumption of non-vocation would be rarely overcome. Similarly a dispensation from an *infamia iuris,* which has given rise to an irregularity *ex defectu,*[70] does not obviate the presumption of the lack of a vocation. Indeed, because of the heinous character of the delicts which produce the penalty of *infamia iuris,* very solid evidence of a complete amendment must be required of one who has contracted an irregularity under this canon. In virtue of canons 968, § 1; 969, § 1; 973, § 3 and 1363, § 1, the judgment of the proper ordinary is decisive in this matter.

b) Moral Purity

No other moral quality is so suggestive of the genuineness of a divine calling as a candidate's purity. Its great value as a sign of vocation flows both from the natural law and positive ecclesiastical law.[71] So incompatible with man's natural but disordered inclinations are the restraints im-

(Murphy: Baltimore, 1896), p. 36: "Innocence of life and integrity of moral character is another mark of a divine vocation, or rather a sign of one's fitness for the ministry, and an indispensable condition for its adequate fulfillment."

[67] Canon 987, 7°.

[68] Canon 984, 5°.

[69] Canon 2293, § 3.

[70] Canon 984, 5°.

[71] Cf. canons 132, § 1; 2358; 2359.

posed by the Church's discipline of celibacy, that it is at once evident that the willingness and the ability of a young man to bind himself sincerely and perpetually to perfect continence are assuredly most persuasive indications of divine predilection.[72] Purity is a gift that inseparably accompanies the grace of a priestly vocation.[73] The Instruction *Quam ingens* identified the ability to keep perfectly chaste as a mark of vocation when it declared that the want of a holy vocation becomes clearly manifest when one acknowledges himself unable to bear that obligation of the priesthood. The lack of vocation is *a fortiori* discernible if a candidate becomes immersed in vicious habits.[74] Whenever there is an instance of a student's notorious moral defection there can be no doubt as to his unsuitability: the ordinary is bound to dismiss the delinquent from the seminary at once. The force of this canon is not restricted to actions but even includes, it would seem, gravely obscene conversations or the reading of salacious books.[75]

Little or no allowance can properly be made for a seminarian's really doubtful capability of observing in the future the law of priestly chastity.[76] Canon 973, § 3, demands posi-

[72] Cf. Mt., XIX, 11.

[73] Cf. Pius XI, ep. encycl. *Ad catholici sacerdotii fastigium*, 20 dec. 1935, II: "Praeclarissimum aliud, pietatique coniunctissimum, catholici sacerdotii ornamentum est ea morum castimonia, quam ut omnino diligenterque observent Latinae Ecclesiae clerici, maioribus Ordinibus initiati, tam gravi iubentur officia, ut, si deliquerint, sacrilegii rei eo ipso evadant."—*AAS*, XXVIII (1936), 24.

[74] § 3, n. 4—*AAS*, XXIII (1931), 126.

[75] Canon 1371: "... praesertim vero statim dimittantur qui forte contra bonos mores aut fidem deliquerint."

[76] Since this is essentially a canonical and not a moral dissertation it has been deemed inappropriate to enter into a detailed consideration of the opinions of various moralists on the duties of a confessor who is faced with the delicate problems here indicated. There is ample room for a study on this question alone, but as a summary guide to those who may be concerned with this perplexing matter we provide the following indications from several renowned canonists and moralists.

Gasparri (*De Sacra Ordinatione*, n. 573) held that one who is

tive arguments in support of fitness, and when an essential constituent of suitability is missing or only doubtfully realized, there remains no alternative except to refuse advancement to Orders. This refusal is not, however, in the nature of a penal measure. It is simply a conclusion drawn from that moral and legal principle which states that an evident

---

habituated in *re turpe solitaria* and wishes nevertheless to advance to any of the Sacred Orders is by that very wish not capable of absolution because in willing to accept Major Orders, although aware of his unfitness for them, he sins gravely. This eminent authority based his opinion on the disposition of such a candidate who knows both that he lacks a quality vitally needed for Orders and at the same time intends to expose himself to the serious danger of future sacrileges.

Even though a penitent of this kind here and now gives signs of contrition that would suffice for the licit absolution of a penitent not preparing for Orders, St. Alphonsus (*Theologia Moralis,* [Lib. III, n. 637]) taught that a *recidivus ordinandus* is unworthy of absolution since he lacks the proved sanctity and strength of character expected of a person destined for the priesthood. Such an unworthy or doubtfully worthy aspirant ought, in this hypothesis, to undergo a period of probation, during which time he would prove to his own satisfaction and to the satisfaction of his prudent confessor or director that lapses no longer occur because the habit has been overcome. —Cf. Pius XI, ep. encycl. *Ad catholici sacerdotii fastigium,* 20 dec. 1935: "...qui, peculiari modo, ad libidinis illecebras sese pronum impertiat, neque iam diu experiendo ostenderit illius dehonestamenta effugere posse...."—*AAS,* XXVIII (1936), 40.

The length of this period of probation is difficult to determine and would depend on the individual's excellent character in other respects together with evidence of serious efforts to grow in virtue by the use of the means suggested by spiritual writers, his confessor or director. Simply his assertion of profound and extraordinary contrition would not suffice. Some writers require an entire year of this probation, others three or four months, but according to Cappello (*Tractatus Canonico-Moralis de Sacramentis,* [II, Pars III, n. 411]) the more common and probable opinion specifies a probationary period of six months.

Ter Haar (*Casus Conscientiae,* [3. ed., Torino, 1944], II, 121), in writing of students in the major seminary, stated that if over a period of years leading to the Subdiaconate, a seminarian falls, v.g., once a month into a fully mortal sin of this kind, there is hardly solid hope that he will later observe perfect continence. The abundant

and grave obligation must be satisfied by the most efficacious means available. The good of religion can regularly be served only by morally worthy priests. It is preferable that a *possibly* genuine divine vocation be frustrated in some individual cases rather than that the good of the Church and of souls (including the aspirant's) be in any way endangered by the admission of those who are unworthy or

---

means of grace in the major seminary; a student's normal progress in the spiritual life; the plentiful protections provided by a properly disciplined seminary schedule—all this ought to make such defections completely, or almost completely, out of the question. If impure in the major seminary, how pure in the ministry?

If one is a candidate, not for Major Orders but rather for tonsure or Minors, and is addicted to *peccata occulta et solitaria,* ordinary signs of contrition could allow his being absolved and so advancing to Minor Orders, provided that it is evident that he sincerely intends to be more assiduous in prayer, mortification and other exercises of piety. Such a seminarian is not yet bound by any ecclesiastical law or vow and so he may readily return to the world if failures continue. —Cf. Gasparri, *De Sacra Ordinatione,* n. 575.

Ter Haar (*Casus Conscientiae,* [loc. cit.]) made a necessary distinction in treating the question of students in the preparatory seminary. Greater latitude is permitted in their case because ample time remains for reform before ordination, and besides, the difficult problems of adolescence must be taken into consideration. But by the latter part of this period of preparatory training, if lapses occur, say, once or twice a month, and the seminarian makes no notable efforts to amend, generally speaking he ought to be urged to discontinue the project of studying for the priesthood.

If a sin with an accomplice has taken place, the confessor should not be satisfied to warn the candidate of the very great seriousness of the offense and its possible scandal, but should even oblige him, under threat of refusal of absolution, to depart from the seminary, especially if it happens more than a single time. This would seem to be a safe rule to observe at whatever stage of a seminary career, whether in the minor or the major seminary. A sin of this kind is so indicative of instability in virtue as to preclude further question of suitability for the priesthood.—Cf. Ter Haar, *Casus Conscientiae,* n. 124. The well-known American moralist, Fr. Connell, has treated this complex and delicate matter briefly but lucidly in the article, "The Seminarian's Confessor," in *The American Ecclesiastical Review,* CXVI (1947), 179-183.

only dubiously qualified. There can, it seems, be no appeal to probabilism, since the selection of suitable priests is primarily for the spiritual welfare of the faithful, and if there is a doubt respecting an ordinand's capacity to remain faithful to his obligation of perfect continency, then the rule *in dubio pars tutior eligenda est*[77] requires his rejection. The argument that is based on the principle that the sacraments operate *ex opere operato* and therefore that the good of the faithful will be safeguarded, is not relevant. It is the intent of ecclesiastical legislation that a candidate have *"mores ordini recipiendo congruentes"* for licit ordination,[78] irrespective of the fact that the Orders, once received, are always validly exercised. If one has a vocation, it is not merely to be *a* priest but to be a *worthy* priest.[79]

In virtue of the sacramental seal a confessor can in no wise use knowledge gained in the administration of penance to guide his actions in the external forum. By the same token the Code excuses confessors from the right to vote whenever a student's admission to Orders or expulsion from a seminary is under consideration.[80] But the decision of a confessor is of profound importance in the matter of vocation in so far as his opinion of a candidate's moral fitness will necessarily have consequence in the external forum. The ordinary and the seminary authorities can judge only such qualities as are externally observable, but a confessor or a spiritual director is able to penetrate deeply into the moral life and conscience of an aspirant, and accordingly discover the indications of vocation, among which the gift of purity

[77] Cf. Noldin, *Summa Theologiae Moralis* (13. ed., 3 vols., Oeniponte, 1921), Vol. I, n. 234.

[78] Canon 974, § 1, 2°.

[79] Canon 973, § 1: "Prima tonsura et ordines illis tantum conferendi sunt . . . quos merito coniicere liceat aliquando dignos futuros esse presbyteros."

[80] Canon 1361, § 3: "Quando agitur de alumno ad ordines admittendo vel e Seminario expellendo, numquam confessariorum votum exquiratur." Cf. Pius XI, ep. encycl. *Ad catholici sacerdotii fastigium*, 20 dec. 1935, *AAS*, XXVIII (1936), 41.

is eminent.[81] The view of Blowick, who denies to the confessor and the spiritual director any discretionary role in the interpretation of divine vocation,[82] is untenable in light of these principles and the authoritative support given them by papal acts. The legally recognized interior element of a vocation is too firmly entrenched in the law to justify an exclusion or even the minimizing of its decisive importance.[83]

Finally, in regard to purity there can be no place for a false charity that would lead a confessor or a spiritual moderator to an indulgent leniency on the plea of a penitent's personal weakness in this matter. The question is very simply one of the ability, in co-operation with grace, to observe perfect chastity. A pronounced fragility in this connection is of itself a coercive mark of no vocation. True charity both to the Church and to the troubled candidate demands that he be not ordained. A seminarian who has proved unchaste in preparing for the priesthood can scarcely be expected to become the subject of a quasi-miracle of grace at the moment of his ordination.[84]

C. OTHER MARKS OF MORAL FITNESS

Also to be sought as signs of moral suitability are those qualities observable only, or at least more usually, in the

[81] Cf. Gasparri, *De Sacra Ordinatione*, n. 118: "Deinde abscondita cordis sui [candidatus] sincere denudet, sinus et recessus conscientiae aperiat suo moderatori, qui hoc modo eius indolem, ingenium, animi propensionem, divinas motiones, incrementa virtutum percipiet....", n. 119: "[in dubio, praesertim in materia castitatis] ... pronuntiandum est pro non-vocatione."; Coronata, *De Sacramentis*, II, n. 51.

[82] *Priestly Vocation*, p. 248.

[83] Cf. S.C. de Sacramentis, instr. *Quam ingens*, 27 dec. 1930, Appendix, Mod. I: "... diligenter re perpensa coram Deo ... experiar ac sentiam a Deo me esse revera vocatum."—*AAS*, XXIII (1931), 127.

[84] Cf. instr. *Quam ingens*, 27 dec. 1930, § 1, n. 3: "... Episcopus seu Ordinarius in perscrutandis moribus eorum qui adscribi petunt sacrae militiae, prae oculis habeat oportet, maxime interesse ut a limine eiiciantur, seu ne ad tonsuram et minores Ordines admittantur ii, qui sacerdotio fungendo non sint apti, seu a Deo non sint vocati."—*AAS*, XXIII (1931), 121; Pius XI, ep. encycl. *Ad catholici sacerdotii fastigium*, 20 dec. 1935—*AAS*, XXVIII (1936), 40-41.

external forum. The general moral complexion of a candidate will regularly become apparent in the searching light of the seminary routine, where daily contact with the seminary staff and fellow seminarians serves to reveal a student's character. Ready obedience to the rules of community life; regularity and promptness in attendance at prescribed exercises; dutiful discharge of assignments; cheerfulness and steadiness of temperament; generosity in the acceptance of the normal inconveniences of seminary life; zeal for all that pertains to the divine cult, the welfare of the Church and the salvation of souls—these considerations must all be carefully weighed by the ministers of vocation, and a proportionate value given each quality if a sound and canonically justified conclusion is to be reached concerning the authenticity of an alleged call.[85]

But any evidence of an excessive desire for personal comfort and ease; such frequent violation of seminary rules as bespeaks a mentality that contemns authority; a noticeable attitude of faultfinding towards the seminary's administration (due allowance made, however, for the seminarian's traditional "*ius murmurandi*"); a marked incompatibility with fellow seminarians,—these and similar character defects give rise to a presumption of non-vocation.

Recreation and sports have a necessary and laudable place in seminary life because of the invaluable role they play in the formation of a well-rounded man, but when a seminarian shows an inclination to make relaxation an end instead of a means, the Holy See has warned authorities to question the genuineness of his vocation.[86] A danger in this regard was

[85] Cf. canon 1371; S.C. de Sacramentis, instr. *Quam ingens*, 27 dec. 1930, § 2, n. 5: "Seminarii moderàtor, diligentissime notitiam de promovendis exquirere curabit ab alumnorum praefectis ... de singularibus nempe vocationis signis, uti sunt pietas, modestia, castitas, de propensione ad sacras functiones.... "—*AAS*, XXIII (1931), 123; Pius X, Motu proprio *Sacrorum antistitum*, 1 sept. 1910—*AAS*, II (1910), 667.

[86] Cf. instr. *Quam ingens*, 27 dec. 1930, § 2, n. 6—*AAS*, XXIII (1931), 123.

singled out by the Sacred Congregation of Studies in a privately circulated recommendation dated January 24, 1928, and reminding seminary officials:

> A reasonable amount of recreation is indispensable in a seminary as a manner of relief, spiritual and mental, to students who grow tired under the burden of their studies, and likewise in order to assist them toward proper physical development. However, sports are a means, not an end in themselves, and therefore ought to be chosen not only with this idea in mind, but also with due consideration for the special nature and general purpose of the seminary itself, which has not been established to turn out athletes who are able to exhibit their skill and prowess before the public on an athletic field. Rather the purpose of a seminary is to turn out athletes who will fight bravely the battles of the Lord.[87]

2. *Mental Suitability*

The probative value of an aspirant's intelligence as a mark of his vocation consists not in his acquired knowledge but in his native capacity for acquiring knowledge. While there is a proportionate relation between these two factors in so far as formal education frequently keeps pace with the natural mental ability, yet the connection is by no means intrinsic and hence no particular stress need be placed upon the degree of one's learning when a possible divine vocation is being weighed. Lacunae in one's formal education can often be supplied for by means of individual scholastic instruction, but innate intellectual capability is a gift of grace and nature within the meaning of the Church's law.[88]

The degree of acumen expected of a candidate for Orders must be uniformly high. Assuredly it is not to be less than the average.[89] Indeed, a somewhat superior intelligence may

[87] Bouscaren, *The Canon Law Digest,* I, 652.

[88] Cf. the decision of the commission of Cardinals, headed by R. Card. Merry del Val, under the date of July 2, 1912—*AAS,* IV (1912), 485.

[89] The standardized intelligence examinations generally available from educators will often prove of assistance in this determination.

fittingly be looked for as an index of a true vocation when one considers the present wide diffusion of education; the struggle being waged for men's minds in the realm of ideas; the ever-present demands of the scholastic discipline in our seminaries. The priest's apostolate is also intellectual in character.[90]

The Code clearly allows some variation in the courses of studies undertaken in the minor seminaries, and proportions their extent and depth to the level of general educational culture and clerical learning proper to that portion of the Church wherein the future priest will exercise his ministry. The measuring rule is the need of the faithful.[91] This degree of adaptation in the scholastic exigencies of preparatory seminaries is an example of the infeasibility of attempting to lay down any hard and fast rule relative to the amount of intellectual aptitude which constitutes an assured mark of a divine vocation. A great deal therefore depends upon the prudent discretion of the ordinary[92] and effective co-operation of the auxiliary ministers of vocation[93] in the exercise of the judgment concerning the sufficient mental capacity of the ordinand. One need not be a genius to have a vocation, nor may one—except perhaps in a most singular instance such as that of the Curé d'Ars or Joseph Cupertino[94]—be a dullard.

As a criterion of the presence of a vocation, the interest of a seminarian in his required studies is as significative as

[90] Cf. Pius X, Motu proprio, *Sacrorum antistitum*, 1 sept. 1910—*AAS*, II (1910), 667-668.

[91] Cf. canon 1364, 3°. Educational requirements have not always been constant. The Council of Trent demanded for tonsure only the ability to read and write joined with a knowledge of the rudiments of the Faith.—Sess. XXIII, *de ref.*, c. 4—Mansi, XXXIII, 142.

[92] Canon 969, § 1: "Nemo ex saecularibus ordinetur, qui iudicio proprii Episcopi non sit necessarius vel utilis ecclesiis dioecesis."

[93] Canon 1371: "E Seminario dimittantur . . . qui in studiis adeo parum proficiant ut spes non affulgeat eos sufficientem doctrinam fore assecuturos . . . ."

[94] Cf. Pius XI, ep. encycl. *Ad catholici sacerdotii fastigium*, 20 dec. 1935, IV—*AAS*, XXVIII (1936), 49.

the ability to learn. When a student is irresponsible in the employment of his time; lackadaisical; given to prolonged, useless or worldly conversations; follows an inclination to read to excess such material as has no pertinence to the seminary curriculum; demonstrates a greater facility (and delight) in memorizing current batting-averages than in remembering necessary theological and philosophical distinctions and principles—such a candidate would certainly render suspect the reality of his vocation. The improper use of intellectual gifts is as sure a gauge of non-vocation as is their lack, and such an abuse, when not amenable to correction, creates a strong presumption against the mental suitability of an ordinand.[95]

3. *Physical Suitability*

The sign of a divine vocation as supplied by physical fitness for the priesthood is stated in the Code in a negative rather than in a positive manner in the canon on irregularities *ex defectu*,[96] which reflects a law substantially unchanged since the epoch of Gregory IX (1227-1241).[97] In virtue of canon 984, 2°, 3°, any defect of body, whether attributable to one's own fault or not, which renders an aspirant incapable of a fitting performance of the sacred functions of the altar produces an irregularity. A narrow acceptation of the provision of this canon would appear to confine the irregularity to such a defect as would impede a safe or becoming discharge of the priest's sacrificial ministry.[98] But the intention of the legislator can hardly

[95] Cf. Leo XIII, ep. encycl. *Depuis le jour*, 8 sept. 1899, nn. 6, 7—*Fontes*, n. 642; S.C. Consist., litt. circ., 16 iul. 1912—*Fontes*, n. 2084; Gasparri, *De Sacra Ordinatione*, n. 116; Stockums, *Vocation to the Priesthood* (translated by J.W. Grundner, Herder: St. Louis, 1937), p. 163.

[96] Canon 984, 2°, 3°.

[97] Cf. Wernz-Vidal, *Ius Canonicum*, IV, n. 239.

[98] Canon 984, 2°: "Corpore vitiati qui secure propter debilitatem, vel decenter propter deformitatem, altaris ministerio defungi non valeant."

be restricted to such a literal interpretation. It seems more consonant with the general tenor of legislation relative to suitability, to extend the force of the canon to any physical deficiency of such a serious nature as would obstruct the successful accomplishment of any of the necessary and often arduous duties of the active ministry. Thus a constitutional weakness or acquired defect so pronounced as to preclude one from a satisfactory discharge of such obligations as preaching; teaching; hearing confessions for even long periods of time; active direction of societies, and other similar tasks, would tend to raise a presumption against physical fitness. It would not be required for this presumption that an irregularity *ex defectu corporis* in the full canonical sense be proved.

Among corporal imperfections clearly constituting such irregularities are blindness, deafness, dumbness, notable lameness demanding the use of a cane, a stomach disorder excluding the use of wine, dwarfness, lack of necessary fingers required in the saying of Mass, and in general any marked bodily deformity that would excite umbrage or wonderment among the faithful.[99] These and similar irregularities that are congenital, are in and of themselves (*per se*) an argument of non-vocation, but some irregularity contracted after birth provides—in theory—no evidence of the lack of a possibly once-existent "vocation". Yet, in the hypothesis of an acquired perpetual irregularity that does not, from the practice of the Roman Curia, admit of dispensation, it is evidently useless to speculate on the existence of a vocation in the irregular one since no ecclesiastical call will issue. An irregularity of itself perpetual but nevertheless admitting of dispensation constitutes only a slight presumption against the presence of a divine vocation. In the case of an irregularity of this type it would be necessary to weigh all the other qualifications of the ordinand, and if his general

[99] Cf. Wernz-Vidal, *Ius Canonicum,* IV, n. 239; Beste, *Introductio in Codicem,* p. 530; S.C.C., *Fabrianen.-Mathelicen.,* 7 sept. 1833—*Fontes,* n. 4048; S.C.C., *Bergomen.,* 27 nov. 1858—*Fontes,* n. 4168; S.C.C., *Pinhelen.,* 16 iun. 1865—*Fontes,* n. 4200.

aptitude was in other respects so convincing as to warrant a petition for a dispensation, then indeed the presence of a vocation might rightfully be indicated, and only if the petition is denied need the defect in question be taken as prevailing evidence of no call to Orders.[100]

In a case of doubt as to whether or not an extant physical defect impedes a licit promotion to Orders, the proper ordinary of the ordinand is competent to pronounce a declaratory sentence.[101] If he decides that an irregularity is present, a petition for a dispensation may be addressed to the Supreme Pontiff to whom is reserved the granting of such dispensations.[102] But if the ordinary is doubtful about the fact of the existence of the irregularity he may dispense, provided that the conditions for a dispensation are verified.[103]

It might be noted that while a clerical seminary is not a military academy, and certainly the priesthood as such does not demand of its members the physical strength and stamina proper to combat officers, yet at least the average condition of good health must surely be found in a student for the priesthood. The regular and searching physical examinations demanded for admission to the seminary or novitiate ought to disclose whether or not a candidate shows adequate corporal endowments. A physical weakling in the seminary is an anomaly.

4. *Right Intention*

The nature of an ordinand's motives in seeking admis-

[100] Cf. Gasparri, *De Sacra Ordinatione*, n. 116; S.C.C., *Comaclen.*, 5 dec. 1863: "... Clericum Iosephum Fogli evidentia ecclesiasticae vocationis signa prae se ferentem ex passa infirmitate tali in tibia defectu laborare, ut genu dextrum inflectere nequeat.... *Pro gratia dispensationis et habilitationis, facto verbo cum Sanctissimo (Die 27 februarii 1864 Sacra, etc. respondit).*"—*Fontes*, n. 4197.

[101] Gasparri, *op. cit.*, n. 254.

[102] Wernz-Vidal, *Ius Canonicum*, IV, n. 239.

[103] Canon 15: "Leges, etiam irritantes et inhabilitantes, in dubio iuris non urgent; in dubio autem facti potest Ordinarius in eis dispensare, dummodo agatur de legibus in quibus Romanus Pontifex dispensare solet."

sion to Orders is of notable interest for those who are obliged to look for the presence of authentic signs of a divine vocation.[104] The emphasis historically placed on this important constituent of suitability for the priesthood has been indicated in the consideration of simoniacal ordination,[105] and the prevailing legislation no less certainly demonstrates a pointed insistence on the propriety of a candidate's intention. Fundamentally, the stress laid by ecclesiastical law on the rightness of one's intention in approaching Orders is rooted in the very character of the priestly office as a ministry for the spiritual good of the Church's members.[106] It is therefore inadmissible that any motive other than the glory of God and the welfare of souls be predominant in the reasons for an aspirant's decision to study for the priesthood. The *finis operantis* must coincide with the *finis operis* if one's motivation is to be perfectly licit.

The credit for the recognition of a right intention as a specific sign of a divine vocation appears to be due to the moralist-canonist Hallier (†1659), who prepared the way for the later juridical development of this doctrine. His teaching on the right intention as a condition precedent to the lawful reception of Orders was of singular clarity.[107]

Hallier's exposition was no doubt greatly influenced by certain pertinent acts of the Council of Trent, which acts, although not expressly describing the intention as a mark of vocation, nevertheless equivalently did so by requiring that the ordinand be moved by a constant and proper will.

[104] Cf. the judgment of the commission of Cardinals appointed by Pope Pius X to examine the work of Joseph Lahitton, *La Vocation Sacerdotale,* given July 2, 1912, 3º—*AAS,* IV (1912), 485.

[105] Cf. *supra,* Chapter V, *Article* 3, A., n. 3.

[106] Cf. canon 948; Wernz-Vidal, *Ius Canonicum,* IV, n. 215; *dictum Gratiani* ad c. 43, C. I, q. 1: "Cetera enim sacramenta unicuique propter se dantur.... Istud solum non propter se solum, sed propter alios datur... ad quorum utilitatem, non solum ut presint, sed etiam ut prosint, sacerdotium datur."

[107] Hallier, Pars I, sect. III, cap. II, n. XXIX: "Alterum divinae vocationis indicium est intentionis rectitudo ac puritas... ob quam aliquis ad sacram ordinationem accedit...."

Thus there were to be admitted into the seminary only those applicants whose qualities offered a solid hope of their unfailing perseverance in the faithful discharge of the sacred ministry.[108] And by the time a candidate was prepared to accept tonsure, the rightness of his intention was expected to be an assured fact, sufficiently evident to permit a probable conjecture that he was duly motivated in his decision. He was to be excluded from initiation into the clerical state if the authorities felt that he sought tonsure merely in order to avoid unpleasant consequences of his remaining a layman, and not to promote God's greater honor.[109]

The Code has incorporated almost verbatim Chapter Eighteen of the twenty-third session (*de ref.*) of the Council of Trent[110] in canon 1363, § 1.[111] The text of this canon indicates the necessity of finding out the candidate's purpose in entering the seminary, to determine if a fruitful and stable dedication to the sacred ministry might properly be anticipated. Lack of a right intention would constitute a likely omen of an unsuccessful future ministry, and when this want of rightness in intention is manifest, the law requires the ordinary to refuse admission to the seminary. A fit motive in desiring the priesthood is an effect of grace operating within the soul, and therefore ministers of vocation should regularly accord intention pre-eminent value as a determinant of the reality of vocation.[112]

[108] Cf. sess. XXIII, *de ref.*, c. 18: "In hoc vero collegio recipiantur ii... quorum indoles et voluntas spem afferat, eos ecclesiasticis ministeriis perpetuo inservituros."—Mansi, XXXIII, 147.

[109] Sess. XXIII, *de ref.*, c. 4: "Prima tonsura non initientur... de quibus probabilis coniectura non sit, eos, non saecularis iudicii fugiendi fraude, sed ut Deo fidelem cultum praestent, hoc vitae genus elegisse."—Mansi, XXXIII, 142.

[110] Mansi, XXXIII, 147.

[111] "In Seminarium ab Ordinario ne admittantur, nisi filii legitimi quorum indoles et voluntas spem afferant eos cum fructu ecclesiasticis ministeriis perpetuo inservituros."

[112] Cf. Pius XI, ep. encycl. *Ad catholici sacerdotii fastigium*, 20 dec. 1935, III: "... ex recta eorum propensione eruitur intentioneque mentis qui sacerdotio inhiant.... Qui ad sacrum huiusmodi institu-

While canon 1363, § 1, exacts of the ordinary the duty of disallowing entry into a seminary to those youths whose will and intention are suspect, analogously canon 992 requires the ordinands themselves, whether secular or religious, to make known to their bishop or religious superior, at a convenient time prior to ordination, their desire to receive Orders.[113] The exact signification of *"propositum"* in canon 992 is not deducible from its context, but cognate provision in the legislation of the Council of Trent, the source of this present law, uses the word *"desiderio"* in connection with a requirement to make known to the bishop one's intention in being ordained.[114]

Consequent upon the revelation of the candidate's intention as called for in canon 992, follows the publication of the banns of ordination as provided for in canon 998, together with the obligation placed upon all the faithful to reveal to ecclesiastical authority any impediment to ordination which they may happen to know.[115] Moreover, the ordinary may ask the pastor publishing the banns to conduct an investigation into the suitability of the aspirant, and the bishop may also, if he judges it advisable, consult still others regarding the character of the ordinand.[116] Thus the candidate's manifestation of his wish initiates a legal process calculated to uncover any deficiencies in requisite fitness, including any

---

tum ea una nobilique de causa contendat ... ad sacerdotale ministerium a Deo vocatur."—*AAS*, XXVIII (1936), 40; S.C. de Prop. Fide, instr. (ad Vic. Ap. Sin.), 18 oct. 1883, § IV, nn. 1, 4—*Fontes*, n. 4903; Leo XIII, ep encycl. *Fin dal principio*, 8 dec. 1902, § 5—*Fontes*, n. 650.

[113] "Omnes tum saeculares tum religiosi ad ordines promovendi per se ipsi vel per alios Episcopo aliive qui Episcopi hac in re vices gerat, suum propositum ante ordinationem opportuno tempore aperiant."

[114] Cf. sess. XXIII, *de ref.*, c. 5—Mansi, XXXIII, 143.

[115] Canon 999: "Omnes fideles obligatione tenentur impedimenta ad sacros ordines, si qua norint, Ordinario vel parocho ante sacram ordinationem revelandi."

[116] Canon 1000.

serious fault in his intention.[117] Whatever may have been the legal force originally intended to be conveyed by *"propositum"* in canon 992, recent instructions pertinent to this canon as correlated with canon 973, §§ 1, 3, point to the Church's preoccupation for certifying the rightness of the intention of the ordinand. The Instruction *Quam ingens,* expressly designed for preventing the acceptance into the sacerdotal office of those who are destitute of a divine vocation,[118] singled out the causes adduced by those who seek a declaration of the nullity of their ordination or a release from the obligations annexed thereto. Of the reasons advanced to support petitions for a process of this kind, the instruction stated that some are *"intimae seu intrinsecae"* as distinguished from the *"extrinsecae."* The latter are concerned with the force and fear brought to bear to compel one to be ordained. The former, intimate or intrinsic reasons, uniformly evince the absence of a right intention in the one ordained. Among these causes alleged to disprove the *"vera voluntas"* required for a canonical ordination are the faulty intentions of leading a more commodious life; of obtaining the honor and esteem associated with the priesthood; of securing imagined financial advantages; of escaping manual labor; of enjoying the privileges and exemp-

---

[117] Cf. S.C. Ep. et Reg., instr. (ad Ep. Hungariae), 28 maii 1896, II: "Episcopi autem, memores gravissimae Apostoli admonitionis: *Manus cito nemini imposueris, neque communicaveris peccatis alienis,* summa cum diligentià explorent num forte sint qui, non vocati a Deo, seipsos sive ob quaestum sive ob ambitionem terrenamque quamcumque cupiditatem ad sacerdotium ecclesiasticumque ministerium intrudant, *quo quidem hominum genere mercenariorum nihil infelicius ac miserius, nihil Ecclesiae Dei calamitosius esse potest."*—*Fontes,* n. 2030.

[118] § 1, n. 1: "Quam ingens Ecclesiae atque animarum saluti detrimentum inferant qui, divina destituti vocatione, sacerdotale ministerium inire praesumunt, angelicis ipsis humeris formidandum, neminem profecto fugit."—*AAS,* XXIII (1931), 120. A similar instruction for religious institutes was issued the following year.—Cf. S.C. de Religiosis, instr. *Quantum Religiones,* 1 dec. 1931—*AAS,* XXIV (1932), 74-81.

tions commonly accorded the clerical state, as immunity from military service; or simply the intention of attaining to an exalted position.[119]

To forestall those seeking ordination with these and related illicit motives, the Instruction *Quam ingens* contains an Appendix listing detailed interrogatories to be answered by the candidate's pastor and by others who may be equally acquainted with the degree of fitness of a student and his intention.[120] The defective intentions mentioned in this directive as frequently presented in processes dealing with the obligations annexed to Orders are such as leave no doubt of their entire incompatibility with an authentic divine call. But there are intentions less clearly indicative of a non-vocation and these can be spoken of as inadequate intentions. Thus, for example, one might desire the priesthood primarily as a means to his personal sanctification, or because he might regard the priesthood as a way to expiate for past offenses against God's laws. These and like sentiments are quite praiseworthy if they be considered in abstraction from the purpose of the priesthood *qua* priesthood, but evidently they have no standing as motives for ordination to a religio-social office instituted for the spiritual welfare of others.[121] The ministers of vocation, whether the ordinary or his delegates, and also the auxiliaries such as the confessors and spiritual directors, if they discern the inadequacy of a candidate's intention, are expected in virtue of their office to probe more carefully into the suspect intention and by pru-

[119] Cf. instr. *Quam ingens*, 27 dec. 1930, § 1, n. 4—*AAS*, XXIII (1931), 121; Pius XI, ep. encycl. *Ad catholici sacerdotii fastigium*, 20 dec. 1935—*AAS*, XXVIII (1936), 40.

[120] Appendix: Mod. I, II, III—*AAS*, XXIII (1931), 127-129.

[121] Cf. canon 948: "Ordo ex Christi institutione clericos a laicis in Ecclesia distinguit ad fidelium regimen et cultus divini ministerium."; Pius XI, ep. encycl. *Ad catholici sacerdotii fastigium*, 20 dec. 1935, I: "Minister Christi sacerdos: divini igitur Redemptoris quasi instrumentum est, ut mirabilem eius operam, quae superna efficacitate universum hominum convictum redintegrans, eum ad excellentiorem cultum traduxit, per tempora persequi valeat."—*AAS*, XXVIII (1936), 10.

dent counsel to direct the will of the aspirant towards the formation of a right intention. If this effort proves unavailing, the student should be dissuaded or deterred from pursuing a goal the real purpose of which he either does not comprehend or ignores.[122]

If the seminarian's ruling intention in preparing for the priesthood is properly to further the glory of God and to promote the spiritual welfare of the faithful,[123] then certain secondary and subordinate intentions, v.g., the desire of personal sanctification, the wish for greater freedom from family distractions, or the seeking of wider opportunities for intellectual development, are fully compatible with the genuineness of his vocation.[124] A right intention, which is the result of a grace enlightening the intellect and strengthening the will, is inextricably joined with the grace itself of a vocation,[125] and when this intention is constant, not capricious; personal, not the outgrowth of undue parental pressure; deeply rooted in the consciousness, not superficial; distinct in its apprehension of the essence and duties of the priesthood—then the rightness of such an intention will normally manifest itself with a clarity that will allow the ministers of vocation to pronounce it a strong sign of the divine call. Finally, the law appeals directly to the conscience of the ordinand for a guarantee of the propriety of his motives.[126]

[122] Cf. Pius XI, ep. encycl. *Ad catholici sacerdotii fastigium,* III: "...non aptos aeque atque indignos, humano nullo habito respectu, pro officio [moderatores] iubeant e sacris Seminarii saeptis, dum tempus est, recedere...."—*AAS,* XXVIII (1936), 41; Stockums, *Vocation to the Priesthood,* p. 126.

[123] Cf. Pius XI, *loc. cit.*—*AAS,* XXVIII (1936), 40.

[124] Cf. Gibbons, *The Ambassador of Christ,* p. 35.

[125] Cf. Nilles, *Commentarius de Vocatione,* p. 50: "[Vocatio est] ... ex illustratione Spiritus sancti, intellectui misericorditer immissa, et ex peculiari Dei impulsu, quo voluntas hominis accendatur et elevetur ad optandum et sibi procurandum bonum adeo excelsum."

[126] Cf. the oath prescribed in the Appendix of the Instruction *Quam ingens,* Mod. I: "Ego subsignatus N.N., cum petitionem Episcopo exhibuerim pro recipiendo ... presbyteratus Ordine, sacra in-

ARTICLE 4. The Juridical Value of Inclination as a Sign of Vocation

A. THE HISTORY OF THE DOCTRINE OF ATTRACTION

Among certain authors who treated canonical-theological matters relative to Sacred Orders, there appeared about the middle of the seventeenth century a tendency to demand of ordinands a subjective attraction for or inclination to the sacerdotal office. This attraction was interpreted by some writers as an indispensable prerequisite for licit ordination. If one lacked such an inclination, it was asserted that he could not be considered as having a divine call.[127] Perpetuated by later authors in substantially the same form, the doctrine that a candidate had to experience a definite propensity to the priesthood was accorded a role of exaggerated importance by Branchereau (1819-1913), who in the closing years of the nineteenth century published a work that defended this view, and he even went so far as practically to identify divine vocation with attraction.[128]

This overemphasis on attraction in effect distorted the subjective and purely interior element of vocation and caused detriment to the correct concept of the external-ec-

---

stante Ordinatione, ac diligenter re perpensa coram Deo, iuramento interposito, testificor in primis, nulla me coactione seu vi, nec ullo impelli timore in recipiendo eodem sacro Ordine, sed ipsum sponte exoptare, ac plena liberaque voluntate eumdem velle, cum experiar ac sentiam a Deo me esse revera vocatum. Fateor mihi plene esse cognita cuncta onera caeteraque ex eodem sacro Ordine dimanantia . . . ."—*AAS*, XXIII (1931), 127; Pius XI, ep. encycl. *Ad catholici sacerdotii fastigium*, 20 dec. 1935, II; III—*AAS*, XXVIII (1936), 23-24; 40-41.

[127] Cf. Hallier, Pars I, sect. II, cap. III, n. XXXIII: "De propensione denique ad vitam ecclesiasticam debitam a parocho, et de praeceptoribus attestationem afferre teneatur . . . ."; n. XXXI: "Quare ex natura rei, in quam nulla cadere potest dispensatio, non potest quis ad tonsuram recipi, qui animum a clericali professione pro eo tempore aversum habeat . . . . " Blowick mentioned other French writers of the same opinion who were contemporaries of Hallier.—Cf. *Priestly Vocation*, p. 59.

[128] Cf. *De la Vocation Sacerdotale*, pp. 183, 248, 260.

clesiastical call by tending to enshroud the entire problem of divine vocation with an unwarranted air of subjectivism and mysticism. This was a distinct disservice both to jurisprudence and to theology.

This author's presentation of the attraction theory was erroneous chiefly in its assertion that one who laid claim to a strong attraction to the priesthood was on that account evidently divinely called and so had a quasi-right to receive ordination. If this error had been widely accepted in the Church, all ordinaries would have been placed in the difficult position either of ordaining virtually anyone who felt an inclination to the sacred ministry, or, in the event of the refusal to do so, of appearing to place oneself against God's will! Obviously an absurd alternative was the logical extension of this fallacious interpretation of the value of attraction.

In a laudable attempt to refute Branchereau's misapprehension, Canon Joseph Lahitton wrote a reply vigorously attacking the entire doctrine of attraction and endeavoring to show that even when (and if) there was such an inclination to the priesthood still it constituted no indication of a divine call. At the same time, Lahitton impugned the notion of antecedent divine vocation by establishing the totality of the vocational concept in the episcopal invitation to Orders.[129] A heated controversy between the adherents of these conflicting opinions reached the attention of Rome. A special Commission of Cardinals upon examining the work of Lahitton approved certain of the author's tenets, especially those wherein he had denied anyone's right to receive Orders before the issuance of the episcopal summons, and had repudiated the identification of vocation to the priesthood with the attraction to it. It is worthy of note that the cautiously phrased judgment of the Cardinals did not rule out inclination as a sign of vocation nor did it weaken the doctrine of anterior divine vocation. The decision simply

[129] Cf. *La Vocation Sacerdotale, passim.* Blowick, in his *Priestly Vocation,* closely followed Lahitton.

affirmed that no one enjoyed, before the episcopal call, any vested right to be ordained, and denied that vocation consisted necessarily in some internal and vague inspiration produced by the Holy Spirit.[130] This judgment brought into proper perspective the vastly important function of the bishop's call in the concept of vocation to the priesthood, and at the same time dissipated the aura of mysticism that had commenced to envelop that legal doctrine.[131]

B. CANONICAL EVALUATION OF ATTRACTION

Canonical commentators and pontifical acts have determined the value of attraction with a clarity and emphasis that allows no vagueness about either its nature or its necessity. Gasparri recognized the divine origin of inclination to the priesthood when he wrote that God does not commonly call men to the sacred ministry without simultaneously giving them an attraction towards it. This propensity is not something sensible, nor does it preclude the possibility of a kind of natural repugnance for the sacrifices and the responsibilities of the priestly office.[132]

The inherent taste or God-given attraction to the sacerdotal life is composed of two constitutive elements: 1) an intellectual conviction of the supreme worth of the priesthood, since one is not apt to seek after a thing for which he does not possess a high regard or which he does not be-

[130] "1° Neminem habere unquam ius ullum ad ordinationem antecedenter ad liberam electionem episcopi. 2° Conditionem, quae ex parte ordinandi debet attendi, quaeque *vocatio sacerdotalis* appellatur, nequaquam consistere, saltem necessario et de lege ordinaria, in interna quadam adspiratione subiecti, seu invitamentis Spiritus Sancti, ad sacerdotium ineundum."—*AAS*, IV (1912), 485.

[131] Coronata was of the opinion that the intention of the Commission was also to dispel any scruple in candidates who, although otherwise canonically qualified for ordination, might nevertheless feel themselves without a divine vocation simply for the reason that they were aware of no sensible attraction to the priesthood.—Cf. *De Sacramentis*, II, p. 60, n. 49, footnote 6.

[132] Cf. *De Sacra Ordinatione*, n. 117; Gibbons, *The Ambassador of Christ*, p. 35.

lieve will satisfy some longing; 2) an inclination in the will to pursue the good (the sacred ministry) presented by the intellectual perception of the desirability, for this individual, of the priesthood.[133] This attraction is not founded on mere sentimentality or emotions; it is a fact to be ascertained by self-examination and by the scrutiny of prudent counselors.[134] Although propensity, as a grace, is an integral part of the divine vocational decree, yet it derives from God only indirectly, that is, through the candidate's native aptitude for the priestly office. His physical, intellectual and moral suitability are gifts of grace and nature,[135] and this suitability establishes such a harmonious relationship with the exercise of the sacred ministry that even the prospective performance of the clerical duties proves an agreeable and attractive thing to a candidate divinely called. God would give no authentic attraction for a state for which one is unsuited.[136]

If attraction is to serve as a sign of vocation it must be of a stable and not of an oscillating character, since a youth who has only a transitory or fluctuating inclination to a state that is of itself unalterable would be unpromising vocational material. That does not mean, however, that an aspirant's desire for or propensity to the priesthood need remain of unvarying intensity. One's consciousness of his esteem for the sacerdotal office, together with his awareness of his natural capacity for its functions, may be more or less vivid from time to time. Evidently this inclination ought

[133] Cf. Gasparri, *De Sacra Ordinatione*, n. 117: "[signum ordinarium vocationis ecclesiasticae est] sensus quidam supernaturalis hominem inclinans ad amplectendum statum clericalem intuitu gloriae Dei et salutis proximorum"; Cappello, *Tractatus Canonico-Moralis de Sacramentis*, II, Pars III, 374.

[134] Cf. Coronata, *De Sacramentis*, II, n. 49; Gasparri, *De Sacra Ordinatione*, n. 118; Gibbons, *The Ambassador of Christ*, p. 32.

[135] Cf. the judgment of the Commission of Cardinals, July 2, 1912, 3°: "Sed e contra, nihil plus in ordinando, ut rite vocetur ab episcopo, requiri quam rectam intentionem simul cum idoneitate in iis gratiae et naturae dotibus reposita . . . ."—*AAS*, IV (1912), 485.

[136] Cf. Many, *Praelectiones de Sacra Ordinatione*, pp. 212-213.

not be absent for any notable period—Gasparri required that it be strong and constant.[137]

Although the above-cited judgment of the Commission of Cardinals stated that an inclination need not always be present with a vocation, nevertheless the great likelihood of its presence was indicated by Pius XI when he wrote the encyclical *Ad catholici sacerdotii fastigium.*[138]

There is an intimate link between inclination to the priesthood and rightness of intention. The latter signifies the motive in the will's desire for the sacred ministry, while the former denotes the moving effect produced on the will by the desirable object inducing the will to tend towards the priesthood as a definite good.[139] This nexus between attraction and intention is supported by the words of Pius XI when he singled out some wrong intentions, and in the same context described as unfit for the sacerdotal state those who have no inclination to the duties inseparably associated with it.[140]

The legislator does not envision a taste for the priesthood as unsusceptible of evaluation in the external forum. Attraction is not some nebulous and impalpable emotion or sentiment. It manifests itself in a tangible and juridically assessable manner. Thus the Instruction *Quam ingens* requires the seminary rector to secure from the members of the seminary staff their observations and conclusions con-

[137] *De Sacra Ordinatione*, n. 117. Cf. S. Romani, *Institutiones Juris Canonici* (Romae, 1944), Vol. II, n. 497: "Haec [vocatio divina] autem est actus quo Deus fidelis animam inclinat, allicit, movet, attrahit suaviter, constanter, fortiter, ad statum clericalem; eam igitur, qui vocatur, ipse intus experitur...."

[138] Cf. III: "Quae quidem ad sacra capessenda munia proclivis inclinatio, uti probe nostis, Venerabiles Fratres, potiusquam ex intimo conscientiae invitamento sensuumque motu, quae interdum deesse possunt, ex recta eorum propensione eruitur intentioneque mentis qui sacerdotio inhiant...."—*AAS*, XXVIII (1936), 40.

[139] Cf. St. Thomas Aquinas, *Summa Theologica*, Ia-IIae, q. 8, a. 1 ad 2um: "Nam nulla potentia prosequitur nisi suum conveniens obiectum."

[140] Cf. ep. encycl. *Ad catholici sacerdotii fastigium*, 20 dec. 1935, III—*AAS*, XXVIII (1936), 40.

cerning the vocational criteria revealed by the conduct of the seminarians, and the manifestation of a propensity is specifically mentioned as one of these signs. Practical norms for discovering the presence of an inclination are provided in the two series of interrogatories annexed to the Instruction.[141]

When Pope Pius XI stated in no uncertain terms that there is no place in a seminary for a young man who does not exhibit a propensity of will for the priesthood, he thus canonized an ordinand's inclination to the ministry as an authentic mark of his divine vocation.[142]

[141] § 2, n. 5—*AAS*, XXIII (1931), 123.

[142] Ep. ap. *Officiorum omnium*, 1 aug. 1922: "Quare non modo in eis [seminariis] locus esse non debet pueris vel adolescentulis, qui nullam ad sacerdotium praeferant propensionem voluntatis . . . ."—*AAS*, XIV (1922), 451. Cf. Pius X, motu propr. *Sacrorum antistitum*, 1 sept. 1910, VII—*Fontes*, n. 689; S.C. de Prop. Fide, instr. (ad Vic. Ap. Sin.), 18 oct. 1883, IV, 1: "Quo vero certiores fiant VV. AA. de bona puerorum inclinatione quos ad hunc numerum eligunt [in seminario] . . . quis admitti peteret . . . illius propensionem, mores, docilitatem probaturi . . . ."—*Fontes*, n. 4903.

CHAPTER VI

THE ECCLESIASTICAL VOCATION CONSIDERED AS A SIGN

A pseudo-Isidorian epistle attributed to Pope Cletus (76-88) and alleged to have been addressed by him to the bishops of Italy, took cognizance of an interdependence of the divine and the ecclesiastical vocations. In it was a commentary on the Scriptural text, "Pray ye therefore the Lord of the harvest, that he send laborers into his harvest,"[1] and it was explained that the seventy disciples were chosen as priests both by the Lord Himself and by the Apostles. It was furthermore asserted that all priests were the successors of these first disciples, and that priests were selected by the Church as well as by God in order that the ministry might be duly perpetuated.[2]

This recognition that the lawful choice of priests was effected conjointly by divine and ecclesiastical activity introduced a precedent and a method thereafter followed in the selection of persons intended for Sacred Orders. Thus Master Rufinus (†1190) in his commentary on the abovementioned (spurious) decree, referred to the mutual activity that took place between the divine and the human elements. "The Apostles", Rufinus wrote, "called the disciples for Christ, through Him and in Him."[3]

The traditionally predominant role occupied by ordinaries in the external summons to the ministry was reaffirmed by the Tridentine Council,[4] and Hallier incorporated this episcopal function into the juridical doctrine regarding the signs of a vocation when he advised ordinands to regard the de-

[1] Luke, X, 2.

[2] C. 2, D. XXI; Jaffé, n. 4.

[3] *Summa Decretorum*, D. XXI.

[4] Cf. sess. XXIII, *de ref.*, c. 16—Mansi, XXXIII, 146.

cision of ecclesiastical superiors as a "divine oracle."[5] The *Cathechism of the Council of Trent* attributed similar preeminence to the judgment of hierarchical authority: "Let no one *take the honour to himself, but he that is called by God as Aaron was;* and they are called by God who are called by the lawful ministers of His Church."[6]

This text in the *Catechism* equivalently asserted that no one is called by God if he is not also called by legitimate ecclesiastical authority, thereby acknowledging the Church's summons as a cogent mark of the presence of a divine vocation. Accordingly, one who is unable to find a bishop or other ordinary who is willing to extend to him the Church's invitation to Orders can in no wise correctly claim that he has a divine vocation to the priesthood, no matter how suitable for the ministry he may otherwise be. *A divine vocation remains always imperfect and at best merely inchoate prior to the ecclesiastical call, and therefore nonacceptance for Orders is juridical proof of no vocation.*[7]

By express provision in the Code the ultimate and authoritative decision concerning the admission of candidates is reserved to the ordinary, for it is he who is charged with determining which clerics are necessary or useful for his diocese,[8] a prerogative that is the natural consequence of the episcopal office.[9] The ample scope of the ordinary's power thus to determine the authenticity of the aspirant's voca-

[5] Hallier, Pars I, sect. III, cap. II, n. 29: "Divinae vocationis argumentum est inculpatus ad ecclesiasticum statum ingressus . . . optimum, ni fallor, et convenientissimum, ut ab examinatorum et episcoporum ore tanquam a divino oraculo pendeas . . . ." Cf. Thomassinus, Pars II, lib. I, cap. XXV, n. 3.

[6] McHugh and Callan, pp. 318-319. Vermeersch interpreted this text, not as applicable to the doctrine regarding the signs, but as abstracting from the need of any antecedent divine vocation.—*Epitome Iuris Canonici*, II, n. 242; *Religious and Ecclesiastical Vocation*, p. 69. Cappello (*Tractatus Canonico-Moralis de Sacramentis*, II [*De Sacra Ordinatione*], n. 374) pointedly took issue with that opinion.

[7] Cf. Innocent XII, const. *Speculatores*, 4 nov. 1694, § 2—*Fontes*, n. 258.

[8] Canon 969, § 1. [9] Cf. canons 334, §1; 335, §1.

tion[10] is a further indication of the primordial influence of the episcopal call in the formation of the adequate concept of vocation. The ordinary (or his delegate) is therefore exclusively competent to judge in the external forum[11] the weight to be accorded the criteria of vocation in each individual case. Ecclesiastical superiors hold God's place on earth in this matter; they alone are authorized to explore and to interpret the divine decrees which concern vocation, for it pertains to the economy of Providence that a subject know the will of God through his canonically constituted superiors.[12]

Because the judgment of the ordinary is finally decisive regarding the point whether or not a candidate will in fact be duly accepted for the priesthood, this judgment is in consequence the chief mark of the genuineness of a vocation. This official acknowledgment that all the other canonical requirements are realized in the ordinand, is itself the most

[10] Cf. canons 973, § 3; 1357, § 2; 1363, § 1; 1371; Leo XIII, ep. *Iampridem,* 6 ian. 1886, § 7: "... nemini dubium esse potest, non aliis quam Episcopis ius munusque esse docendi et instituendi iuvenes, quos Deus singulari beneficio ex hominibus assumit, ut sint ministri sui ac dispensatores mysteriorum suorum."—*Fontes,* n. 593. The extent of the authority of religious superiors is analogous but it is modified according to the norms of particular constitutions.—Cf. canons 501, § 1; 970; 992; 993; 995, § 1.

[11] The judgment of the spiritual director or confessor is of correspondingly great importance in the internal forum. Cf. Pius X, motu propr. *Sacrorum antistitum,* 1 sept. 1910, VII: "Videant ergo moderatores disciplinae ac pietatis, quam de se quisque spem iniiciant alumni, introspiciantque singulorum quae sit indoles; utrum suo ingenio plus aequo indulgeant, aut spiritus profanos videantur sumere; sintne ad parendum dociles, in pietatem proni, de se non alte sentientes, disciplinae retinentes; rectone sibi fine proposito, an humanis ducti rationibus ad sacerdotii dignitatem contendant; utrum denique convenienti vitae sanctimonia doctrinaeque polleant; aut certe, si quid horum desit, sincero promptoque animo conentur acquirere."—*Fontes,* n. 689; Pius XI, ep. encycl. *Ad catholici sacerdotii fastigium,* 20 dec. 1935, III—*AAS,* XXVIII (1936), 39.

[12] Cf. Tanquerey, *Synopsis Theologiae Moralis et Pastoralis,* III, n. 814; Gibbons, *The Ambassador of Christ,* p. 40.

noteworthy and certain sign of a divine vocation. And so in the practical order the bishop's favorable decision must satisfy any and all doubts concerning the reality of the call. Since an ordinary represents the Church when he issues an invitation to the priesthood, obviously divine help can scarcely be wanting to him who, by virtue of his office, understands best the needs of his diocese.[13] The episcopal judgment, however, remains essentially human, and accordingly is not beyond the pale of fallibility.

Acceptance by the bishop can never serve as a substitute for the other marks that concur to evince the needed suitability. In other words, an ecclesiastical summons does not confer any radical fitness for the ministry. This is evident both from the tenor of canon 973, § 3,[14] and from the purpose of the Instruction *Quam ingens,* which obliges the ministers of vocation to search out diligently the signs of the vocation in question before they may give the ecclesiastical call.[15]

It is to be noted moreover that the external summons to Orders is never so conclusive a sign of the presence of a divine vocation as to permit one licitly to accept ordination even though he is conscious that he lacks a right intention, or that he is devoid of that sanctity which is proportioned to the exigencies of the priesthood, or that he is subject to an occult irregularity. It is for this reason that the internal forum, open only to the scrutiny of confessors and spiritual directors, is of surpassing moment in the determination of one's vocation. The ecclesiastical call is morally without

[13] Cf. Many, *Praelectiones de Sacra Ordinatione,* p. 216.

[14] "Episcopus sacros ordines nemini conferat quin ex positivis argumentis moraliter certus sit de eius canonica idoneitate; secus non solum gravissime peccat, sed etiam periculo sese committit alienis communicandi peccatis."

[15] § 1, n. 1: "... qui [sacerdotes], etsi probare non valeant se vi aut gravi metu fuisse adactos ad sacros Ordines suscipiendos, tamen ex iis quae in actis deducuntur, aperte ostendunt, se fuisse praepostero modo in sacram militiam adlectos, seu non satis fuisse exploratam vocationem ...."—*AAS,* XXIII (1931), 120.

effect or meaning if the divine call is in reality not present.[16]

The admission to Orders can be licitly granted by the competent ecclesiastical authority only if and when that grant is based upon persuasive evidence of the existence of an antecedent divine vocation. An aspirant's complete canonical suitability, the result of his God-given vocation, will foretoken an exact, holy and fruitful exercise of the sacerdotal ministry.[17]

[16] Cf. St. Thomas Aquinas, *Summa Theologica*, IIa-IIae, q. 185, a. 2 ad 2um; Stockums, *Vocation to the Priesthood*, p. 81.

[17] Cf. S.C. de Sacramentis, instr. *Quam ingens*, 27 dec. 1930, § 1, n. 2—*AAS*, XXIII (1931), 121; Pius XI, ep. encycl. *Ad catholici sacerdotii fastigium*, 20 dec. 1935, III—*AAS*, XXVIII (1936), 40; Gasparri, *De Sacra Ordinatione*, n. 117.

CONCLUSIONS

1. The constitutive elements of the adequate concept of a priestly vocation: a special call from God, the due qualities of soul, mind and body in the subject of sacred ordination, and the express invitation from the Church, can be found among the earliest references in the Decretal Law.

2. The antecedent divine call obtains its complement and perfecting element from the Church's official invitation to Orders, so that the two vocations thus coalesce to produce the adequate concept of a vocation to the priesthood.

3. The juridical doctrine which holds that vocation consists in an anterior divine call which is manifested through certain marks in the external (and sacramental) forum, and which achieves its completion through the external call to Orders, is a post-Tridentine development. Its immediate basis is found in the Tridentine Council's laws on the Sacrament of Orders and on the regulations established by it for the institution of clerical seminaries.

4. The use of *"indicia"* in canon 1353 strengthens the theory of antecedent divine vocation as an entity evinced through signs.

5. The right to give the external call to Orders, i.e., the Church's official admission of the ordinand, was originally shared by others with the ordinary, but this right in time became the exclusive prerogative of the bishop. This evolution was crystallized in the enactments of the Council of Trent.

6. The unwarranted emphasis which during previous centuries was placed on the interior aspect of a sacerdotal vocation was rectified both by the judgment of the Commission of Cardinals in 1912 and by the doctrine proposed in subsequent pontifical acts.

7. The doctrine of attraction is amply supported by contemporary jurisprudence.

8. The tenor of canon 973, § 1, as compared with § 3 of the same canon indicates that the legislator demands greater certainty of the presence of a divine vocation for the licit conferring of Major Orders than for the lawful bestowal of ordination in the more remote degrees which successively lead to the ultimate full reception of the Sacrament of Orders.

9. The opinion which holds that there is a divine vocation to the priesthood prior to and really distinct from the external call, enjoys greater favor of the law than the opinion held, for instance, by Vermeersch, which denies the reality of any antecedent divine vocation and identifies it simply with the episcopal summons.

10. The phrase *"ecclesiastica vocatio"* in canon 1353 is used synonymously with the phrase *"divina vocatio"* in the same canon and with the word *"vocatio"* in canon 1357, § 2.

11. The right to receive ordination rests upon an antecedent divine vocation only in so far as this divine vocation is completed by the call of the bishop to Orders. The signs of a vocation therefore have no juridical value anterior to the external call, since fitness for the priesthood is accepted in the law of the ecclesiastical society only through the ordinary's decision. For this reason the episcopal call is the *formal* element in the concept of vocation.

12. Since the exterior summons is the completion of the interior divine call, the former does not really indicate a divine vocation if no complete canonical suitability on the part of the candidate is in fact present. But, if an unfit aspirant is summoned by the competent ecclesiastical authority (even with a conscious unlawfulness on the part of the bishop), then in virtue of the issued call the candidate is to be juridically regarded as called also by God.

13. The authority granted by the law to confessors and spiritual moderators in the determination of the authenticity of one's vocation is commensurate with the discretionary power accorded by the law to superiors who judge suitability only in the external forum.

BIBLIOGRAPHY

Sources

Acta Apostolicae Sedis, Commentarium Officiale, Romae, 1909—.

Acta et Decreta Concilii Plenarii Americae Latinae in Urbe Celebrati, A.D. MDCCCXCIX, Romae, 1902.

Acta Sanctae Sedis, 41 vols., Romae, 1865-1908.

Bouscaren, T.L., *The Canon Law Digest*, 2 vols., Milwaukee: Bruce, 1934-1943.

Bruns, Hermann Theodor, *Canones Apostolorum et Conciliorum Saeculorum IV-VII*, 2 vols., Berolini, 1839.

Catechism of the Council of Trent for Parish Priests, ed. by J.A. McHugh and C. J. Callan, New York, 1923.

Codex Iuris Canonici Pii X Pontificis Maximi iussu digestus Benedicti Papae XV auctoritate promulgatus, Romae, 1917.

Codicis Iuris Canonici Fontes, cura Emi Petri Card. Gasparri editi, 9 vols., Romae (postea Civitate Vaticana): Typis Polyglottis Vaticanis, 1923-1939. Vols. VII-IX, ed. cura et studio Emi Iustiniani Card. Serédi.

Corpus Iuris Canonici, Editio Lipsiensis 2., 2 vols., Richter-Friedberg, Lipsiae, 1879-1881.

Corpus Scriptorum Ecclesiasticorum Latinorum, Editum consilio et impensis Academiae Litterarum Caesareae Vindobonensis, Vindobonae, apud Geroldi Filium, 1866—.

Decretales D. Gregorii Papae IX suae integritati una cum glossis restitutae, ad exemplar Romanum diligenter recognitae, Venetiis, 1591.

Decretum Gratiani emendatum et notationibus illustratum una cum glossis, Gregorii XIII, Pont. Max., iussu editum, 2 vols., Venetiis, 1591.

Jaffé, P., *Regesta Pontificum Romanorum ab condita Ecclesia ad annum post Christum natum, 1198*, Editionem secundam correctam et auctam auspiciis Gulielmi Wattenbach curaverunt S. Loewenfeld, F. Kaltenbrunner, P. Ewald, 2 vols. in 1.

Kirch, C., *Enchiridion Fontium Historiae Ecclesiasticae Antiquae*, 4. ed., Friburgi-Brisgoviae, 1923.

Liber Sextus Decretalium D. Bonifacii Papae VIII, Clementis Papae V Constitutiones, Extravagantes tum Viginti D. Ioannis Papae XXII tum Communes. Haec omnia cum suis glossis integritati restituta, et ad exemplar Romanum diligenter recognita, Venetiis, 1591.

Mansi, I. D., *Sacrorum Conciliorum Nova et Amplissima Collectio*, 53 vols. in 60, Paris, Leipzig, Arnhem, 1901-1927.

Potthast, A., *Regesta Pontificum Romanorum inde ab anno post Christum natum 1198 ad annum 1304*, 2 vols., Berolini, 1874-1875.

Schema Codicis Iuris Canonici, ed. cum notis Petri Card. Gasparri, Romae, 1912.

Authors

Abelly, L., *Sacerdos Christianus*, Vesontione, 1838.

Alphonsus de Liguori, St., *Theologia Moralis*, 4 vols., ed. cura et studio P. Leonardi Gaudé, Romae: Typis Polyglottis Vaticanis, 1905-1912.

Barbosa, A., *Collectanea Doctorum in Varia Concilii Tridentini Decreta et Canones*, Lugduni, 1656.

Beste, U., *Introductio in Codicem*, Collegeville, Minn.: St. John's Abbey Press, 1938.

Blat, A., *Commentarium Textus Codicis Iuris Canonici*, 5 vols. in 7, Lib. II, Pars II-III, 3. ed., Romae: Collegio "Angelico", 1938.

Blowick, J., *Priestly Vocation*, Dublin: M.H. Gill and Son, Ltd., 1932.

Bouscaren, T. L.—Ellis, A. C., *Canon Law—A Text and Commentary*, Milwaukee: Bruce, 1946.

Cappello, F., *Summa Iuris Publici Ecclesiastici*, 5. ed., Romae: Typis Pontificiae Universitatis Gregorianae, 1943.

———, *Tractatus Canonico-Moralis de Sacramentis*, 3 vols. in 6, Vol. II, Pars III, *De Sacra Ordinatione*, Romae: Marietti, 1935.

Davis, H., *Moral and Pastoral Theology*, 4. ed., 4 vols., London: Sheed and Ward, 1943.

Fagnanus, P., *Commentaria in Quinque Libros Decretalium*, 5 vols. in 3, Coloniae Allobrogum, 1759.

Garrigou-Lagrange, R., *De Gratia*, Romae: Marietti, 1946.

Gasparri, P., *Tractatus Canonicus de Sacra Ordinatione*, 2 vols., Parisiis, 1893.

Gibbons, J. Card., *The Ambassador of Christ*, Baltimore: Murphy, 1896.

Hallier, F., *De Sacris Electionibus et Ordinationibus ex Antiquo et Novo Ecclesiae Usu*, apud J.P. Migne, *Theologiae Cursus Completus*, Vol. XXIV, Parisiis, 1860.

Hefele, C., *Histoire des Conciles*, Traduction Française par H. Leclercq sur le deuxième Edition Allemand, 10 vols. in 19, Paris: Letouzey et Ané, 1907-1938.

Hervé, J.M., *Manuale Theologiae Dogmaticae*, 4 vols., Vol. III, 18. ed., Westminster, Md.: Newman, 1943.

Hummelauer, F. de, *Commentarius in Numeros*, Paris, 1899.

Hurtaud, F. J., *La Vocation au Sacerdoce*, 2. ed., Paris, 1911.

Knabenbauer, J., *Commentarius in Evangelium secundum Ioannem*, Paris, 1904.

Lagrange, M.J., *Evangile selon Saint Marc,* Paris, 1911.
Lahitton, J., *La Vocation Sacerdotale,* nouvelle éd., Paris, 1913.
Liddell, H. G., *Greek-English Lexicon,* 8. ed., New York, 1897.
Many, S., *De Sacra Ordinatione,* Parisiis, 1905.
Maupied, *Juris Canonici Universi Compendium,* 2 vols., Paris: Migne, 1863.
Migne, J.P., *Patrologiae Cursus Completus, Series Latina,* 221 vols., Parisiis, 1844-1855.
———, *Patrologiae Cursus Completus, Series Graeca,* 161 vols., Parisiis, 1857-1866.
Nilles, N., *Commentarius de Vocatione ad Statum Ecclesiasticum,* Oeniponte: Pustet, 1892.
Noldin, H., *Summa Theologiae Moralis,* 13. ed., 3 vols., Oeniponte, 1921.
Olier, J.J., *Traité des Saints Ordres,* apud J.P. Migne, *Oeuvres Completes,* Paris, 1856.
Prat, F., *La Théologie de Saint Paul,* Paris 1908.
Prümmer, D., *Manuale Iuris Canonici,* 6. ed., Friburgi-Brisgoviae: Herder, 1933.
Raymundus de Pennafort, S., *Summa,* Veronae, 1744.
Reiffenstuel, A., *Jus Canonicum Universum,* 5 vols. in 7, Parisiis, 1864-1870.
Ryan, G. A., *Principles of Episcopal Jurisdiction,* The Catholic University of America Canon Law Studies, n. 120, Washington, D.C.: The Catholic University of America Press, 1939.
Regatillo, E., *Ius Sacramentarium,* 2 vols., Santander: Sal Terrae, 1945-1946.
Rufinus, *Summa Decretorum,* ed. H. Singer, Paderborn, 1902.
Schmalzgrueber, F., *Jus Ecclesiasticum Universum,* 5 vols. in 12, Romae, 1843-1845.
Stockums, W., *Vocation to the Priesthood,* translated by J.W. Grundner, St. Louis: Herder, 1937.
Thomas Aquinas, St., *Summa Theologica,* 6 vols., Taurinorum Augustae: Marietti, 1938.
———, *Commentaria in Omnes S. Pauli Apostoli Epistolas,* 2 vols., Taurinorum Augustae: Marietti, 1917.
Thomassinus, L., *Vetus et Nova Ecclesiae Disciplina,* 10 vols., Magontiaci, 1787.
Tanquerey, A., *Synopsis Theologiae Moralis et Pastoralis,* 3 vols., 5. ed., New York, 1907-1908.
Ter Haar, Franciscus, *Casus Conscientiae,* 3. ed., Torino, 1944.
Toso, A., *Ad Codicem Juris Canonici Commentaria Minora,* 5 vols., Vol. I, 2. ed., 1921; Vols. II-V, 1922-1927, Romae: Marietti.
Van Espen, Z.B., *Jus Ecclesiasticum Universum,* 10 vols., Venetiis, 1769.

Vermeersch, A., *Religious and Ecclesiastical Vocation*, translated from the Latin by Joseph G. Kempf, St. Louis: Herder, 1925.

———, *Theologiae Moralis, Principia, Responsa, Consilia*, 4 vols., Vol. III, Lib. II, *De Ordine*, 4. ed., 1948, Roma: Typis Pontificiae Universitatis Gregorianae.

Vermeersch, A.—Creusen, J., *Epitome Iuris Canonici*, 5 ed., 3 vols., Mechliniae: Dessain, 1933-1936.

Wernz, F. X., *Ius Decretalium*, 3. ed., 6 vols., Romae et Prati, 1913-1915.

Wernz, F.X.—Vidal, P., *Ius Canonicum*, 7 vols. in 8, Romae: Apud Aedes Universitatis Gregorianae, 1923-1938.

Periodical

American Ecclesiastical Review, The (*The Ecclesiastical Review*, Vol. XXXIII, July [1905]-Vol. CIX, December [1943]), Philadelphia, 1889-1943; Baltimore, 1944—

Index

BIOGRAPHICAL NOTE

Aidan Carr was born September 14, 1914, in Galveston, Texas. He attended parochial and public schools in Washington, D.C. and the Swavely Preparatory School at Manassas, Virginia. In September, 1933, he entered George Washington University, and the following fall enrolled in the Law School of National University at Washington, from which he was graduated in June, 1937. He was admitted to the practice of law before the Bar of the District of Columbia in March, 1938. In August of that year he entered the novitiate of the Order of Friars Minor Conventual, and after making temporary vows began the philosophical course at the Major Seminary of the Conventual Franciscans, St. Anthony-on-Hudson, Rensselaer, New York. After the completion of philosophy he commenced theology at Le Grand Séminaire de St. Sulpice in Montreal, Canada. Ordained to the priesthood in Springfield, Mass., January 13, 1945, he returned the following fall to the Sulpician Seminary in Montreal, from which he obtained the Doctorate in Sacred Theology in June, 1946. In September of the same year he enrolled in the School of Canon Law of the Catholic University of America, and was granted the degree of the Baccalaureate in Canon Law in June, 1947, and of the Licentiate in Canon Law in June, 1948.

CANON LAW STUDIES *

1. FRERIKS, REV. CELESTINE A., C. PP. S., J. C. D., Religious Congregations in Their External Relations, 121 pp., 1916.
2. GALLIHER, REV. DANIEL M., O.P., J.C.D., Canonical Elections, 117 pp., 1917.
3. BORKOWSKI, REV. AURELIUS L., O.F.M., J.C.D., De Confraternitatibus Ecclesiasticis, 136 pp., 1918.
4. CASTILLO, REV. CAYO, J.C.D., Disertación Historico-Canonica sobre la Potestad del Cabildo en Sede Vacante o Impedida del Vicario Capitular, 99 pp., 1919 (1918).
5. KUBELBECK, REV. WILLIAM J., S.T.B., J.C.D., The Sacred Penitentiaria and Its Relation to Faculties of Ordinaries and Priests, 129 pp., 1918.
6. PETROVITS, REV. JOSEPH, J.C., S.T.D., J.C.D., The New Church Law on Matrimony, X-461 pp., 1919.
7. HICKEY, REV. JOHN J., S.T.B., J.C.D., Irregularities and Simple Impediments in the New Code of Canon Law, 100 pp., 1920.
8. KLEKOTKA, REV. PETER J., S.T.B., J.C.D., Diocesan Consultors, 179 pp., 1920.
9. WANENMACHER, REV. FRANCIS, J.C.D., The Evidence in Ecclesiastical Procedure Affecting the Marriage Bond, 1920 (Printed 1935).
10. GOLDEN, REV. HENRY FRANCIS, J.C.D., Parochial Benefices in the New Code, IV-119 pp., 1921 (Printed 1925).
11. KOUDELKA, REV. CHARLES J., J.C.D., Pastors, Their Rights and Duties According to the New Code of Canon Law, 211 pp., 1921.
12. MELO, REV. ANTONIUS, O.F.M., J.C.D., De Exemptione Regularium, X-188 pp., 1921.
13. SCHAAF, REV. VALENTINE THEODORE, O.F.M., S.T.B., J.C.D., The Cloister, X-180 pp. 1921.
14. BURKE, REV. THOMAS JOSEPH, S.T.D., J.C.D., Competence In Ecclesiastical Tribunals, IV-117 pp., 1922.
15. LEECH, REV. GEORGE LEO, J.C.D., A Comparative Study of the Constitution "Apostolicae Sedis" and the "Codex Juris Canonici," 179 pp., 1922.
16. MOTRY, REV. HUBERT LOUIS, S.T.D., J.C.D., Diocesan Faculties According to the Code of Canon Law, II-167 pp., 1922.

* All published numbers are available from the Catholic University of America Press, 620 Michigan Ave., N.E. Washington 17, D.C., except the following: Nos. 1-114 inclusive, 116, 118, 120, 121, 122, 123, 136, 153, 162, 182, and 198. But the following numbers, now reissued, are obtainable from *The Jurist*, The Catholic University of America, Washington 17, D.C., namely: nos. 5, 7, 11, 17, 18, 19, 26, 28, 30, 31, 34, 42, 44, 51, 52 and 61.

17. Murphy, Rev. George Lawrence, J.C.D., Delinquencies and Penalties in the Administration and the Reception of the Sacraments, IV-121 pp., 1923.
18. O'Reilly, Rev. John Anthony, S.T.B., J.C.D., Ecclesiastical Sepulture in the New Code of Canon Law, II-129 pp., 1923.
19. Michaicka, Rev. Wenceslaus Cyril, O.S.B., J.C.D., Judicial Procedure in Dismissal of Clerical Exempt Religious, 107 pp., 1923.
20. Dargin, Rev. Edward Vincent, S.T.B., J.C.D., Reserved Cases According to the Code of Canon Law, IV-103 pp., 1924.
21. Godfrey, Rev. John A., S.T.B., J.C.D., The Right of Patronage According to the Code of Canon Law, 153 pp., 1924.
22. Hagedorn, Rev. Francis Edward, J.C.D., General Legislation on Indulgences, II-154 pp., 1924.
23. King, Rev. James Ignatius, J.C.D., The Administration of the Sacraments to Dying Non-Catholics, V-141 pp., 1924.
24. Winslow, Rev. Francis Joseph, O.F.M., J.C.D., Vicars and Prefects Apostolic, IV-149 pp., 1924.
25. Correa, Rev. Jose Servelion, S.T.L., J.C.D., La Potestad Legislativa de la Iglesia Catolica, IV-127 pp., 1925.
26. Dugan, Rev. Henry Francis, A.M., J.C.D., The Judiciary Department of the Diocesan Curia, 87 pp., 1925.
27. Keller, Rev. Charles Frederick, S.T.B., J.C.D., Mass Stipends, 167 pp., 1925.
28. Paschang, Rev. John Linus, J.C.D., The Sacramentals According to the Code of Canon Law, 129 pp., 1925.
29. Piontek, Rev. Cyrillus, O.F.M., S.T.B., J.C.D., De Indulto Exclaustrationis necnon Saecularizationis, XIII-289 pp., 1925.
30. Kearney, Rev. Richard Joseph, S.T.B., J.C.D., Sponsors at Baptism According to the Code of Canon Law, IV-127 pp., 1925.
31. Bartlett, Rev. Chester Joseph, A.M., LL.B., J.C.D., The Tenure of Parochial Property in the United States of America, V-108 pp., 1926.
32. Kilker, Rev. Adrian Jerome, J.C.D., Extreme Unction, V-425 pp., 1926.
33. McCormick, Rev. Robert Emmett, J.C.D., Confessors of Religious, VIII-266 pp., 1926.
34. Miller, Rev. Newton Thomas, J.C.D., Founded Masses According to the Code of Canon Law, VII-93 pp., 1926.
35. Roelker, Rev. Edward G., S.T.D., J.C.D., Principles of Privilege According to the Code of Canon Law, XI-166 pp., 1926.
36. Bakalarczyk, Rev. Richardus, M.I.C., J.U.D., De Novitiatu, VIII-208 pp., 1927.
37. Pizzuti, Rev. Lawrence, O.F.M., J.U.L., De Parochis Religiosis, 1927. (Not Printed.)

38. BLILEY, REV. NICHOLAS MARTIN, O.S.B., J.C.D., Altars According to the Code of Canon Law, XIX-132 pp. 1927.
39. BROWN, MR. BRENDAN FRANCIS, A.B., LL.M., J.U.D., The Canonical Juristic Personality with Special References to its Status in the United States of America, V-212 pp., 1927.
40. CAVANAUGH, REV. WILLIAM THOMAS, C.P., J.U.D., The Reservation of the Blessed Sacrament, VIII-101 pp., 1927.
41. DOHENY, REV. WILLIAM J., C.S.C., A.B., J.U.D., Church Property: Modes of Acquisition, X-118 pp., 1927.
42. FELDHAUS, REV. ALOYSIUS H., C.PP.S., J.C.D., Oratories, IX-141 pp., 1927.
43. KELLY, REV. JAMES PATRICK, A.B., J.C.D., The Jurisdiction of the Simple Confessor, X-208 pp., 1927.
44. NEUBERGER, REV. NICHOLAS J., J.C.D., Canon 6 or the Relation of the Codex Juris Canonici to the Preceding Legislation, V-95 pp., 1927.
45. O'KEEFE, REV. GERALD MICHAEL, J.C.D., Matrimonial Dispensations, Powers of Bishops, Priests and Confessors, VIII-232 pp., 1927.
46. QUIGLEY, REV. JOSEPH A.M., A.B., J.C.D., Condemned Societies, 139 pp., 1927.
47. ZAPLOTNIK, REV. JOHANNES LEO, J.C.D., De Vicariis Foraneis, X-142 pp., 1927.
48. DUSKIE, REV. JOHN ALOYSIUS, A.B., J.C.D., The Canonical Status of the Orientals in the United States, VIII-196 pp., 1928.
49. HYLAND, REV. FRANCIS EDWARD, J.C.D., Excommunication, Its Nature, Historical Development and Effects, VIII-181 pp., 1928.
50. REINMANN, REV. GERALD JOSEPH, O.M.C., J.C.D., The Third Order Secular of Saint Francis, 201 pp., 1928.
51. SCHENK, REV. FRANCIS J., J.C.D., The Matrimonial Impediments of Mixed Religion and Disparity of Cult, XVI-318 pp., 1929.
52. COADY, REV. JOHN JOSEPH, S.T.D., J.U.D., A.M., The Appointment of Pastors, VIII-150 pp., 1929.
53. KAY, REV. THOMAS HENRY, J.C.D., Competence in Matrimonial Procedure, VIII-164 pp., 1929.
54. TURNER, REV. SIDNEY JOSEPH, C.P., J.U.D., The Vow of Poverty, XLIX-217 pp., 1929.
55. KEARNEY, REV. RAYMOND A., A.B., S.T.D., J.C.D., The Principles of Delegation, VII-149 pp., 1929.
56. CONRAN, REV. EDWARD JAMES, A.B., J.C.D., The Interdict, V-163 pp., 1930.
57. O'NEILL, REV. WILLIAM H., J.C.D., Papal Rescripts of Favor, VII-218 pp., 1930.
58. BASTNAGEL REV. CLEMENT VINCENT, J.U.D., The Appointment of Parochial Adjutants and Assistants, XV-257 pp., 1930.

59. Ferry, Rev. William A., A.B., J.C.D., Stole Fees, V-136 pp., 1930.
60. Costello, Rev. John Michael, A.B., J.C.D., Domicile and Quasi-Domicile, VII-201 pp., 1930.
61. Kremer, Rev. Michael Nicholas, A.B., S.T.B., J.C.D., Church Support in the United States, VI-136 pp., 1930.
    la intención en la aplicación de la Santa Misa, VII-104 pp., 1931.
62. Angulo, Rev. Luis, C.M., J.C.D., Legislación de la Iglesia sobre
63. Frey, Rev. Wolfgang Norbert, O.S.B., A.B., J.C.D., The Act of Religious Profession, VIII-174 pp., 1931.
64. Roberts, Rev. James Brendan, A.B., J.C.D., The Banns of Marriage, XIV-140 pp., 1931.
65. Ryder, Rev. Raymond Aloysius, A.B., J.C.D., Simony, IX-151 pp., 1931.
66. Campagna, Rev. Angelo, Ph. D., J.U.D., Il Vicario Generale del Vescovo, VII-205 pp., 1931.
67. Cox, Rev. Joseph Godfrey, A.B., J.C.D., The Administration of Seminaries, VI-124 pp., 1931.
68. Gregory, Rev. Donald J., J.U.D., The Pauline Privilege, XV-165 pp., 1931.
69. Donohue, Rev. John F., J.C.D., The Impediment of Crime, VII-110 pp., 1931.
70. Dooley, Rev. Eugene A., O.M.I., J.C.D., Church Law on Sacred Relics, IX-143 pp., 1931.
71. Orth, Rev. Clement Raymond, O.M.C., J.C.D., The Approbation of Religious Institutes, 171 pp., 1931.
72. Pernicone, Rev. Joseph M., A.B., J.C.D., The Ecclesiastical Prohibition of Books, XII-267 pp., 1932.
73. Clinton Rev. Connell, A.B., J.C.D., The Paschal Precept, IX-108 pp., 1932.
74. Donnelly, Rev. Francis B., A.M., S.T.L., J.C.D., The Diocesan Synod, VIII-125 pp., 1932.
75. Torrente, Rev. Camilo, C.M.F., J.C.D., Las Procesiones Sagradas, V-145 pp., 1932.
76. Murphy, Rev. Edwin J., C.PP.S., J.C.D., Suspension Ex Informata Conscientia, XI-122 pp., 1932.
77. MacKenzie, Rev. Eric F., A.M., S.T.L., J.C.D., The Delict of Heresy in its Commission, Penalization, Absolution, VII-124 pp., 1932.
78. Lyons, Rev. Avitus E., S.T.B., J.C.D., The Collegiate Tribunal of First Instance, XI-147 pp., 1932.
79. Connolly, Rev. Thomas A., J.C.D., Appeals, XI-195 pp., 1932.
80. Sangmeister, Rev. Joseph V., A.B., J.C.D., Force and Fear as Precluding Matrimonial Consent, V-211 pp., 1932.
81. Jaeger, Rev. Leo A., A.B., J.C.D., The Administration of Vacant

and Quasi-Vacant Episcopal Sees in the United States, IX-229 pp., 1932.

82. RIMLINGER, REV. HERBERT T., J.C.D., Error Invalidating Matrimonial Consent, VII-79 pp., 1932.
83. BARRETT, REV. JOHN D. M., S.S., J.C.D., A Comparative Study of the Councils of Baltimore and the Code of Canon Law, X-223 pp., 1932.
84. CARBERRY, REV. JOHN J., PH. D., S.T.D., J.C.D., The Juridical Form of Marriage, X-177 pp., 1934.
85. DOLAN, REV. JOHN L., A.B., J.C.D., The Defensor Vinculi, XII-157 pp., 1934.
86. HANNAN, REV. JEROME D., A.M., S.T.D., LL.B., J.C.D., The Canon Law of Wills, IX-517 pp., 1934.
87. LEMIEUX, REV. DELISE A., A.M., J.C.D., The Sentence in Ecclesiastical Procedure, IX-131 pp., 1934.
88. O'ROURKE, REV. JAMES J., A.B., J.C.D., Parish Registers, VII-109 pp., 1934.
89. TIMLIN, REV. BARTHOLOMEW, O.F.M., A.M., J.C.D., Conditional Matrimonial Consent, X-381 pp., 1934.
90. WAHL, REV. FRANCIS X., A.B., J.C.D., The Matrimonial Impediments of Consanguinity and Affinity, VI-125 pp., 1934.
91. WHITE, REV. ROBERT J., A.B., LL.B., S.T.B., J.C.D., Canonical Ante-Nuptial Promises and the Civil Law, VI-152 pp., 1934.
92. HERRERA, REV. ANTONIO PARRA, O.C.D., J.C.D., Legislación Eclesiástica sobra el Ayuno y la Abstinencia, XI-191 pp., 1935.
93. KENNEDY, REV. EDWIN J., J.C.D., The Special Matrimonial Process in Cases of Evident Nullity, X-165 pp., 1935.
94. MANNING, REV. JOHN J., A.B., J.C.D., Presumption of Law in Matrimonial Procedure, XI-111 pp., 1935.
95. MOEDER, REV. JOHN M., J.C.D., The Proper Bishop for Ordination and Dimissorial Letters, VII-135 pp., 1935.
96. O'MARA, REV. WILLIAM A., A.B., J.C.D., Canonical Causes for Matrimonial Dispensations, IX-155 pp., 1935.
97. REILLY, REV. PETER, J.C.D., Residence of Pastors, IX-81 pp., 1935.
98. SMITH, REV. MARINER T., O.P., S.T.LR. J.C.D., The Penal Law for Religious, VII-169 pp., 1935.
99. WHALEN, REV. DONALD W., A.M., J.C.D., The Value of Testimonial Evidence in Matrimonial Procedure, XIII-297 pp., 1935.
100. CLEARY, REV. JOSEPH F., J.C.D., Canonical Limitations on the Alienation of Church Property, VIII-141 pp., 1936.
101. GLYNN, REV. JOHN C., J.C.D., The Promoter of Justice, XX-337 pp., 1936.
102. BRENNAN, REV. JAMES H., S.S., M.A., S.T.B., J.C.D., The Simple Convalidation of Marriage, VI-135 pp., 1937.

103. Brunini, Rev. Joseph Bernard, J.C.D., The Clerical Obligations of Canons 139 and 142, X-121 pp., 1937.
104. Connor, Rev. Maurice, A.B., J.C.D., The Administrative Removal of Pastors, VIII-159 pp., 1937.
105. Guilfoyle, Rev. Merlin Joseph, J.C.D., Custom, XI-144 pp., 1937.
106. Hughes, Rev. James Austin, A.B., A.M., J.C.D., Witnesses in Criminal Trials of Clerics, IX-140 pp., 1937.
107. Jansen, Rev. Raymond J., A.B., S.T.L., J.C.D., Canonical Provisions for Catechetical Instruction, VII-153 pp., 1937.
108. Kealy, Rev. John James, A.B., J.C.D., The Introductory Libellus in Church Court Procedure, XI-121 pp., 1937.
109. McManus, Rev. James Edward, C.SS.R., J.C.D., The Administration of Temporal Goods in Religious Institutes, XVI-196 pp., 1937.
110. Moriarty, Rev. Eugene James, J.C.D., Oaths in Ecclesiastical Courts, X-115 pp., 1937.
111. Rainer, Rev. Eligius George, C.SS.R., J.C.D., Suspension of Clerics, XVII-249 pp., 1937.
112. Reilly, Rev. Thomas F., C.SS.R., J.C.D., Visitation of Religious, VI-195 pp., 1938.
113. Moriarty, Rev. Francis E., C.SS.R., J.C.D., The Extraordinary Absolution from Censures, XV-334 pp., 1938.
114. Connolly, Rev. Nicholas P., J.C.D., The Canonical Erection of Parishes, X-132 pp., 1938.
115. Donovan, Rev. James Joseph, J.C.D., The Pastor's Obligation in Pre-nuptial Investigation, XII-322 pp., 1938.
116. Harrigan, Rev. Robert J., M.A., S.T.B., J.C.D., The Radical Sanation of Invalid Marriages, VIII-208 pp., 1938.
117. Boffa, Rev. Conrad Humbert, J.C.D., Canonical Provisions for Catholic Schools, VII-211 pp., 1939.
118. Parsons, Rev. Anscar John, O.M. Cap., J.C.D., Canonical Elections, XII-236 pp., 1939.
119. Reilly, Rev. Edward Michael, A.B., J.C.D., The General Norms of Dispensation, XII-156 pp., 1939.
120. Ryan, Rev. Gerald Aloysius, A.B., J.C.D., Principles of Episcopal Jurisdiction, XII-172 pp., 1939.
121. Burton, Rev. Francis James, C.S.C., A.B., J.C.D., A Commentary on Canon 1125, X-222 pp., 1940.
122. Miaskiewicz, Rev. Francis Sigismund, J.C.D., Supplied Jurisdiction According to Canon 209, XII-340 pp., 1940.
123. Rice, Rev. Patrick William, A.B., J.C.D., Proof of Death in Prenuptial Investigation, VIII-156 pp., 1940.
124. Anglin, Rev. Thomas Francis, M.S., J.C.D., The Eucharistic Fast, VIII-183 pp., 1941.

125. COLEMAN, REV. JOHN JEROME, J.C.D., The Minister of Confirmation, VI-153 pp., 1941.
126. DOWNS, REV. JOHN EMMANUEL, A.B., J.C.D., The Concept of Clerical Immunity, XI-163 pp., 1941.
127. ESSWEIN, REV. ANTHONY ALBERT, J.C.D., Extrajudicial Penal Powers of Ecclesiastical Superiors, X-144 pp., 1941.
128. FARRELL, REV. BENJAMIN FRANCIS, M.A., S.T.L., J.C.D., The Rights and Duties of the Local Ordinary Regarding Congregations of Women Religious of Pontifical Approval, V-195 pp., 1941.
129. FEENEY, REV. THOMAS JOHN, A.B., S.T.L., J.C.D., Restitutio in Integrum, VI-169 pp., 1941.
130. FINDLAY, REV. STEPHEN WILLIAM, O.S.B., A.B., J.C.D., Canonical Norms Governing the Deposition and Degradation of Clerics, XVII-279 pp., 1941.
131. GOODWINE, REV. JOHN, A.B., S.T.L., J.C.D., The Right of the Church to Acquire Property, VIII-119 pp., 1941.
132. HESTON, REV. EDWARD LOUIS, C.S.C., PH.D., S.T.D., J.C.D., The Alienation of Church Property in the United States, XII-222 pp., 1941.
133. HOGAN, REV. JAMES JOHN, A.B., S.T.L., J.C.D., Judicial Advocates and Procurators, XIII-200 pp., 1941.
134. KEALY, REV. THOMAS M., A.B., LITT.B., J.C.D., Dowry of Women Religious, IX-152 pp., 1941.
135. KEENE, REV. MICHAEL JAMES, O.S.B., J.C.D., Religious Ordinaries and Canon 198, V-164 pp., 1941.
136. KERIN, REV. CHARLES A., S.S., M.A., S.T.B., J.C.D., The Privation of Christian Burial, XVI-279 pp., 1941.
137. LOUIS, REV. WILLIAM FRANCIS, M.A., J.C.D., Diocesan Archives, X-101 pp., 1941.
138. MCDEVITT, REV. GILBERT JOSEPH, A.B., J.C.D., Legitimacy and Legitimation, X-247 pp., 1941.
139. MCDONOUGH, REV. THOMAS JOSEPH, A.B., J.C.D., Apostolic Administrators, X-217 pp., 1941.
140. MEIER, REV. CARL ANTHONY, A.B., J.C.D., Penal Administrative Procedure Against Negligent Pastors, XI-240 pp., 1941.
141. SCHMIDT, REV. JOHN ROGG, A.B., J.C.D., The Principles of Authentic Interpretation in Canon 17 of the Code of Canon Law, XII-331 pp., 1941.
142. SLAFKOSKY, REV. ANDREW LEONARD, A.B., J.C.D., The Canonical Episcopal Visitation of the Diocese, X-197 pp., 1941.
143. SWOBODA, REV. INNOCENT ROBERT, O.F.M., J.C.D., Ignorance in Relation to the Imputability of Delicts, IX-271 pp., 1941.
144. DUBE, REV. ARTHUR JOSEPH, A.B., J.C.D., The General Principles for the Reckoning of Time in Canon Law, VIII-299 pp., 1941.

145. McBride, Rev. James T., A.B., J.C.D., Incardination and Excardination of Seculars, XX-585 pp., 1941.
146. Krol, Rev. John T., J.C.D., The Defendant in Ecclesiastical Trials, XII-207 pp., 1942.
147. Comyns, Rev. Joseph J., C.SS.R., A.B., J.C.D., Papal and Episcopal Administration of Church Property, XIV-155 pp., 1942.
148. Barry, Rev. Garrett Francis, O.M.I., J.C.D., Violation of the Cloister, XII-260 pp., 1942.
149. Bolduc, Rev. Gatien, C.S.V., A.B., S.T.L., J.C.D., Les Etudes dans les Religions Cléricales, VIII-155 pp., 1942.
150. Boyle, Rev. David John, M.A., J.C.D., The Juridic Effects of Moral Certitude on Pre-Nuptial Guarantees, XII-188 pp., 1942.
151. Canavan, Rev. Walter Joseph, M.A., Litt.D., J.C.D., The Profession of Faith, XII-143 pp., 1942.
152. Desrochers, Rev Bruno, A.B., Ph.L., S.T.B., J.C.D., Le Premier Concile Plénier de Québec et le Code de Droit Canonique, XIV-186 pp., 1942.
153. Dillon, Rev. Robert Edward, A.B., J.C.D., Common Law Marriage, X-148 pp., 1942.
154. Dodwell, Rev. Edward John, Ph.D., S.T.B., J.C.D., The Time and Place for the Celebration of Marriage, X-156 pp., 1942.
155. Donnellan, Rev. Thomas Andrew, A.B., J.C.D., The Obligation of the Missa pro Populo, VII-131 pp., 1942.
156. Eltz, Rev. Louis Anthony, A.B., J.C.D., Cooperation in Crime, XII-208 pp., 1942.
157. Gass, Rev. Sylvester Francis, M.A., J.C.D., Ecclesiastical Pensions, XI-206 pp., 1942.
158. Guiniven, Rev. John Joseph, C.SS.R., J.C.D., The Precept of Hearing Mass, XIV-188 pp., 1942.
159. Gulczynski, Rev. John Theophilus, J.C.D., The Desecration and Violation of Churches, X-126 pp., 1942.
160. Hammill, Rev. John Leo, M.A., J.C.D., The Obligations of the Traveler According to Canon 14, VIII-204 pp., 1942.
161. Haydt, Rev. John Joseph, A.B., J.C.D., Reserved Benefices, XI-148 pp., 1942.
162. Huser, Rev. Roger John, O.F.M., A.B., J.C.D., The Crime of Abortion in Canon Law, XII-187 pp., 1942.
163. Kearney, Rev. Francis Patrick, A.B., S.T.L., J.C.D., The Principles of Canon 1127, X-162 pp., 1942.
164. Linahen, Rev. Leo James, S.T.L., J.C.D., De Absolutione Complicis in Peccato Turpi, V-114 pp., 1942.
165. McCloskey, Rev. Joseph Aloysius, A.B., J.C.D., The Subject of Ecclesiastical Law According to Canon 12, XVII-246 pp., 1942.
166. O'Neill, Rev. Francis Joseph, C.SS.R., J.C.D., The Dismissal of Religious in Temporary Vows, VIII-220 pp., 1942.

167. Prince, Rev. John Edward, A.B., S.T.B., J.C.D., The Diocesan Chancellor, X-136 pp., 1942.
168. Riesner, Rev. Albert Joseph, C.SS.R., J.C.D., Apostates and Fugitives from Religious Institutes, IX-168 pp., 1942.
169. Stenger, Rev. Joseph Bernard, J.C.D., The Mortgaging of Church Property, 186 pp., 1942.
170. Waldron, Rev. Joseph Francis, A.B., J.C.D., The Minister of Baptism, XII-197 pp., 1942.
171. Willett, Rev. Robert Albert, J.C.D., The Probative Value of Documents in Ecclesiastical Trials, X-124 pp., 1942.
172. Woeber, Rev. Edward Martin, M.A., J.C.D., The Interpellations XII-161 pp., 1942.
173. Benko, Rev. Matthew Aloysius, O.S.B., M.A., J.C.D., The Abbot *Nullius*, XVI-148 pp., 1943.
174. Christ, Rev. Joseph James, M.A., S.T.L., J.C.D., Dispensation from Vindicative Penalties, XIV-285 pp., 1943.
175. Clancy, Rev. Patrick M. J., O.P., A.B., S.T.Lr., J.C.D., The Local Religious Superior, X-229 pp., 1943.
176. Clarke, Rev. Thomas James, J.C.D., Parish Societies, XII-147 pp., 1943.
177. Connolly, Rev. John Patrick, S.T.L., J.C.D., Synodal Examiners and Parish Priest Consultors, X-223 pp., 1943.
178. Drumm, Rev. William Martin, A.B., J.C.D., Hospital Chaplains, XII-175 pp., 1943.
179. Flanagan, Rev. Bernard Joseph, A.B., S.T.L., J.C.D., The Canonical Erection of Religious Houses, X-147 pp., 1943.
180. Kelleher, Rev. Stephen Joseph, A.B., S.T.B., J.C.D., Discussions with Non-Catholics: Canonical Legislation, X-93 pp., 1943.
181. Lewis, Rev. Gordian, C.P., J.C.D., Chapters in Religious Institutes, XII-169 pp., 1943.
182. Marx, Rev. Adolph, J.C.D., The Declaration of Nullity of Marriages Contracted Outside the Church, X-151 pp., 1943.
183. Matulenas, Rev. Raymond Anthony, O.S.B., A.B., J.C.D., Communication, a Source of Privileges, XII-225 pp., 1943.
184. O'Leary, Rev. Charles Gerard, C.SS.R., J.C.D., Religious Dismissed After Perpetual Profession, X-213 pp., 1943.
185. Power, Rev. Cornelius Michael, J.C.D., The Blessing of Cemeteries, XII-231 pp., 1943.
186. Shuhler, Rev. Ralph Vincent, O.S.A., J.C.D., Privileges of Religious to Absolve and Dispense, XII-195 pp., 1943.
187. Ziolkowski, Rev. Thaddeus Stanislaus, A.B., J.C.D., The Consecration and Blessing of Churches, XII-151 pp., 1943.
188. Heneghan, Rev. John Joseph, S.T.D., J.C.D., The Marriages

of Unworthy Catholics: Canons 1065 and 1066, XVI-213 pp., 1944.

189. CARROLL, REV. COLEMAN FRANCIS, M.A., S.T.L., J.C.L., Charitable Institutions.
190. CIESLUK, REV. JOSEPH EDWARD, PH.B., S.T.L., J.C.D., National Parishes in the United States, VI-178 pp., 1944.
191. COBURN, REV. VINCENT PAUL, A.B., J.C.D., Marriages of Conscience, XII-172 pp., 1944.
192. CONNORS, REV. CHARLES PAUL, C.S.SP., A.B., J.C.D., Extra-Judicial Procurators in the Code of Canon Law, X-94 pp., 1944.
193. COYLE, REV. PAUL RAYMOND, A.B., J.C.D., Judicial Exceptions, X-142 pp., 1944.
194. FAIR, REV. BARTHOLOMEW FRANCIS, A.B., S.T.L. J.C.D., The Impediment of Abduction, XII-122 pp., 1944.
195. GALLAGHER, REV. THOMAS RAPHAEL, O.P., A.B., S.T.LR., J.C.D., The Examination of the Qualities of the Ordinand, X-166 pp., 1944.
196. GANNON, REV. JOHN MARK, S.T.L., J.C.D., The Interstices Required for the Promotion to Orders, XII-100 pp., 1944.
197. GOLDSMITH, REV. J. WILLIAM, B.C.S., S.T.L., J.C.D., The Competence of Church and State Over Marriages—Disputed Points, X-128 pp., 1944.
198. GOODWINE, REV. JOSEPH GERARD, A.B., S.T.B., J.C.D., The Reception of Converts, XIV-326 pp., 1944.
199. KOWALSKI, REV. ROMUALD EUGENE, O.F.M., A.B., J.C.D., Sustenance of Religious Houses of Regulars, X-174 pp., 1944.
200. MCCOY, REV. ALAN EDWARD, O.F.M., J.C.D., Force and Fear in Relation to Delictual Imputability and Penal Responsibility, XII-160 pp., 1944.
201. MCDEVITT, REV. VINCENT JOHN, PH.B., S.T.L., J.C.L., Perjury.
202. MARTIN, REV. THOMAS OWEN, PH.D., S.T.D., J.C.D., Adverse Possession, Prescription and Limitation of Actions: The Canonical "Praescriptio," XX-208 pp., 1944.
203. MIKLOSOVIC, REV. PAUL JOHN, A.B., J.C.L., Attempted Marriages and Their Consequent Juridic Effects.
204. MUNDY, REV. THOMAS MAURICE, A.B., S.T.L., J.C.D., The Union of Parishes, X-164 pp., 1944.
205. O'DEA, REV. JOHN COYLE, A.B., J.C.D., The Matrimonial Impediment of Nonage, VIII-126 pp., 1944.
206. OLALIA, REV. ALEXANDER AYSON, S.T.L., J.C.D., A Comparative Study of the Christian Constitution of States and the Constitution of the Philippine Commonwealth, XII-136 pp., 1944.
207. POISSON, REV. PIERRE-MARIE, C.S.C., A.B., PH.L., TH.L., J.C.L., Droits Patrimoniaux des Maisons et des Eglises Religieuses.

208. STADALNIKAS, REV. CASIMIR JOSEPH, M.I.C., J.C.D., Reservation of Censures, X-141 pp., 1944.
209. SULLIVAN, REV. EUGENE HENRY, S.T.L., J.C.D., Proof of the Reception of the Sacraments, X-165 pp., 1944.
210. VAUGHAN, REV. WILLIAM EDWARD, J.C.D., Constitutions for Diocesan Courts, X-210 pp., 1944.
211. PARO, REV. GINO, S.T.D., J.C.D., The Right of Papal Legation, X-221 pp., 1944.
212. BALZER, REV. RALPH FRANCIS, C.P., J.C.D., The Computation of Time in a Canonical Novitiate, X-227 pp., 1945.
213. DOUGHERTY, REV. JOHN WHELAN, A.B., S.T.L., J.C.D., De Inquisitione Speciali, XII-195 pp., 1945.
214. DZIOB, REV. MICHAEL WALTER, J.C.D., The Sacred Congregation for the Oriental Church, XII-181 pp., 1945.
215. EIDENSCHINK, REV. JOHN ALBERT, O.S.B., B.A., J.C.D., The Election of Bishops in the Letters of Pope Gregory the Great, VIII-200 pp., 1945.
216. GILL, REV. NICHOLAS, C.P., J.C.D., The Spiritual Prefect in Clerical Religious Houses of Study, X-140 pp., 1945.
217. HYNES, REV. HARRY GERARD, S.T.L., J.C.D., The Privileges of Cardinals, XII-183 pp., 1945.
218. MCDEVITT, REV. GERALD VINCENT, S.T.L., J.C.D., The Renunciation of an Ecclesiastical Office, XIV-179 pp., 1945.
219. MANNING, REV. JOSEPH LEROY, J.C.D., The Free Conferral of Offices, VII-116 pp., 1945.
220. MEYER, REV. LOUIS G., O.S.B., A.B., S.T.B., J.C.D., Alms-gathering by Religious, XII-163 pp., 1945.
221. O'DONNELL, REV. CLETUS FRANCIS, M.A., J.C.D., The Marriage of Minors, XII-268 pp., 1945.
222. PRUNSKIS, REV. JOSEPH, J.C.D., Comparative Law, Ecclesiastical and Civil, in Lithuanian Concordat, X-161 pp., 1945.
223. SWEENEY, REV. FRANCIS PATRICK, C.SS.R., J.C.D., The Reduction of Clerics to the Lay State, X-199 pp., 1945.
224. VOGELPOHL, REV. HENRY JOHN, J.C.D., The Simple Impediments to Holy Orders, XVI-190 pp., 1945.
225. BROCKHAUS, REV. THOMAS AQUINAS, O.S.B., J.C.D., Religious Who Are Known as *Conversi*, X-127 pp., 1945.
226. GRIESE, REV. ORVILLE NICHOLAS, S.T.D., J.C.D., Marriage and the Procreation of Offspring, XVI-224 pp., 1945.
227. BOUDREAUX, REV. WARREN LOUIS, J.C.D., The "*ab acatholicis nati*" of Canon 1099, § 2, XII-110 pp., 1946.
228. BOWE, REV. THOMAS JOSEPH, A.B., J.C.D., Religious Superioresses, VIII-206 pp., 1946.
229. DIEDERICHS, REV. MICHAEL FERDINAND, S.C.J., J.C.D., The Juris-

diction of the Latin Ordinaries over their Oriental Subjects, XIV-153 pp., 1946.

230. DINGMAN, REV. MAURICE JOHN, A.B., S.T.L., J.C.L., The Plaintiff in Contentious Trials.
231. FRISON, REV. BASIL, C.M.F., M.MUS. J.C.D., The Retroactivity of Law, X-221 pp., 1946.
232. GALVIN, REV. WILLIAM ANTHONY, M.A., J.C.D., The Administrative Transfer of Pastors, XII-288 pp., 1946.
233. GORACY, REV. JOSEPH C., J.C.L., The Diriment Matrimonial Impediment of Major Orders.
234. HALE, REV. JOSEPH FRANCIS, M.A., S.T.L., J.C.D., The Pastor of Burial, X-247 pp., 1946.
235. HENRY, REV. JOSEPH ARTHUR, A.B., J.C.D., The Mass and Holy Communion: Interritual Law, XII-138 pp., 1946.
236. LINENBERGER, REV. HERBERT, C.PP.S., J.C.D., The False Denunciation of an Innocent Confessor, VIII-205 pp., 1946.
237. LOWRY, REV. JAMES MARTIN, A.B., J.C.D., Dispensation from Private Vows, XII-216 pp., 1946.
238. LYNCH, REV. GEORGE EDWARD, A.B., S.T.L., J.C.D., Coadjutors and Auxiliaries of Bishops, X-107 pp., 1946.
239. LYNCH, REV. TIMOTHY, M.S.SS.T., J.C.D., Contracts between Bishops and Religious Congregations, XIII-232 pp., 1946.
240. MCCLUNN, REV. JUSTIN DAVID, A.B., S.T.L., J.C.D., Administrative Recourse, VII-142 pp., 1946.
241. LOHMULLER, REV. MARTIN NICHOLAS, A.B., J.C.D., The Promulgation of Law, XII-140 pp., 1947.
242. MCGRATH, REV. JAMES, A.B., J.C.D., The Privilege of the Canon, XII-156 pp., 1946.
243. MARBACH, REV. JOSEPH FRANCIS, A.B., J.C.D., Marriage Legislation for the Catholics of the Oriental Rites in the United States and Canada, XIV-314 pp., 1946.
244. SHIMKUS, REV. BERNARD ALOYSIUS, A.B., J.C.L., The Determination and Transfer of Rite.
245. SMITH, REV. VINCENT MICHAEL, A.B., S.T.L., J.C.L., Ignorance Affecting Matrimonial Consent.
246. WACHTRLE, REV. PAUL ANTHONY, A.B., J.C.L., The Baptism of the Children of Non-Catholics.
247. CROTTY, REV. MATTHEW M., J.C.D., The Recipient of First Holy Communion, X-142 pp., 1947.
248. EAGLETON, REV. GEORGE, J.C.D., The Quinquennial Faculties, Formula IV, XIV-199 pp., 1947.
249. GIBBONS, REV. MARION L., C.M., LL.B., J.C.D., Domicile of the Wife Unlawfully Separated from Her Husband, XIV-171 pp., 1947.

250. KELLY, REV. BERNARD M., S.T.L., J.C.D., The Functions Reserved to Pastors, IX-141 pp., 1947.
251. KILCULLEN, REV. THOMAS J., LL.M., J.C.D., The Collegiate Moral Person as Party Litigant, X-150 pp., 1947.
252. LAFONTAINE, REV. GERMAIN J., W.F., J.C.D., Relations Canoniques entre Le Missionnaire et Ses Superieurs, X-117 pp., 1947.
253. LANE, REV. LORAS T., A.B., S.T.L., J.C.D., Matrimonial Procedure in the Ordinary Court of Second Instance, XVI-184 pp., 1947.
254. LOVER, REV. JAMES F., C.SS.R., J.C.D., The Master of Novices, X-168 pp., 1947.
255. MCNICHOLAS, REV. TIMOTHY J., J.C.L., The *Septimae Manus* Witness.
256. MAROSITZ, REV. JOSEPH J., M.S.C., J.C.D., Obligations and Privileges of Religious Promoted to the Episcopal or Cardinalitial Dignities, XII-180 pp., 1947.
257. MURPHY, REV. FRANCIS J., A.B., J.C.D., Legislative Powers of the Provincial Council, XII-158 pp., 1947.
258. O'BRIEN, REV. ROMAEUS W., O.CARM., J.C.D., The Provincial Superior in Religious Orders of Men, X-294 pp., 1947.
259. PFALLER, REV. BENEDICT A., O.S.B., J.C.D., The *Ipso facto* Effected Dismissal of Religious, XII-225 pp., 1947.
260. POPEK, REV. ALPHONSE S., M.A., J.C.D., The Rights and Obligations of Metropolitans, XX-460 pp., 1947.
261. RISTUCCIA, REV. BERNARD J., C.M., J.C.D., Quasi-Religious, XVI-318 pp., 1947.
262. SONNTAG, REV. NATHANIEL L., O.F.M.CAP., J.C.D., Censorship of Special Classes of Books, XII-147 pp., 1947.
263. STADLER, REV. JOSEPH N., J.C.D., Frequent Holy Communion, X-158 pp., 1947.
264. SZAL, REV. IGNATIUS J., J.C.D., The Communication of Catholics with Schismatics, XII-217 pp., 1947.
265. WAGNER, REV. URBAN S., O.F.M.CONV., J.C.D., Parochial Substitute Vicars and Supplying Priests, IX-126 pp., 1947.
266. QUINN, REV. JOSEPH, M.A., J.C.D., Documents Required for the Reception of Orders, XII-207 pp., 1948.
267. BENNINGTON, REV. JAMES CLEMENT, A.B., J.C.L., The Recipient of Confirmation.
268. BLAHER, REV. DAMIAN JOSEPH, O.F.M., A.B., J.C.L., The Ordinary Processes in Causes of Beatification and Canonization.
269. CLUNE, REV. ROBERT BELL, B.A., J.C.L., The Judicial Interrogation of the Parties.
270. COURTEMANCHE, REV. BASIL F., B.A., J.C.L., The Total Simulation of Matrimonial Consent.

271. DLOUHY, REV. MAUR JOHN, O.S.B., A.B., J.C.L., The Ordination of Exempt Religious.
272. DONOVAN, REV. JOHN THOMAS, PH.B., S.T.L., J.C.D., The Clerical Obligations of Canons 138 and 140, XII-209 pp., 1948.
273. FREKING, REV. FREDERICK W., A.B., S.T.B., J.C.L., The Canonical Installation of Pastors.
274. FULTON, REV. THOMAS B., J.C.L., Prenuptial Investigation.
275. GODLEY, REV. JAMES P., J.C.L., The Time and the Place for the Celebration of Mass.
276. KANE, REV. THOMAS A., A.B., B.S., J.C.D., Jurisdiction of Patriarchs of the Major Sees in Antiquity and in the Middle Ages, XII-111 pp., 1948.
277. KENNEDY, REV. ANDREW A.; J.C.L., The Annual Pastoral Report to the Local Ordinary.
278. KONRAD, REV. JOSEPH GEORGE, J.C.L., Transfer of Religious.
279. KRESS, REV. ALPHONSE, J.C.L., Contumacy in Ecclesiastical Trials.
280. MCCARTNEY, REV. MARCELLUS ANTHONY, O.F.M., M.A., J.C.L., Faculties of Regular Confessors.
281. MCCASLIN, REV. EDWARD PATRICK, M.A., S.T.L., J.C.L., The Division of Parishes.
282. MCELROY, REV. FRANCIS J., A.B., J.C.L., The Privileges of Bishops.
283. QUINN, REV. STEPHEN, M.S.SS.T., J.C.D., Relation between the Local Ordinary and Religious of Diocesan Approval, XII-153 pp., 1948.
284. SCHNEIDER, REV. EDELHARD LOUIS, S.D.S., M.A., J.C.D., The Status of Secularized Ex-Religious Clerics, X-155 pp., 1948.
285. THOMPSON, REV. CHESTER J., A.B., J.C.L., The Simple Removal from Office.
286. O'BRIEN, REV. KENNETH R., A.B., J.C.D., The Nature of Support of Diocesan Priests in the United States, XVI-162 pp., 1949.
287. METZ, REV. JOHN E., S.T.L., J.C.D., The Recording Judge in the Ecclesiastical Collegiate Tribunal, X-130 pp., 1949.
288. REINHARDT, REV. MARION J., S.T.L., J.C.L., The Rogatory Commission.
289. ORTEGA UHINK, REV. JUAN, S.J., J.C.L., De Delicto Sollicitationis.
290. CASEY, REV. JAMES V., J.C.L., A Study of Canon 2222, § 1.
291. ALLGEIER, REV. JOSEPH L., J.C.L., The Canonical Obligation of Preaching in Parish Churches.
292. CAHILL, REV. DANIEL R., J.C.L., The Custody of the Holy Eucharist.
293. CARR, REV. AIDAN, O.F.M.CONV., S.T.D., J.C.L., LL.B., Vocation to the Priesthood: Its Canonical Concept.

294. KNOPKE, REV. ROCH F., O.F.M., J.C.L., Reverential Fear in Matrimonial Cases in Asiatic Countries: Rota Cases.
295. LAVELLE, REV. HOWARD D., J.C.L., The Obligation of Holding Sacred Missions in Parishes.
296. MICKELLS, REV. ANTHONY B., J.C.L., The Constitutive Elements of Parishes.
297. NOONE, REV. JOHN J., J.C.L., Nullity in Judicial Acts.
298. SHEEHAN, REV. DANIEL E., J.C.L., The Minister of Holy Communion.
299. STATKUS, REV. FRANCIS J., J.C.L., The Minister of the Last Sacraments.
300. COOK, REV. JOHN P., J.C.L., Ecclesiastical Communities and Their Ability to Induce Legal Customs.
301. FAZZALARO, REV. FRANCIS J., J.C.L., The Place for the Hearing of Confessions.
302. HANNAN, REV. PHILIP M., J.C.L., The Canonical Concept of *Congrua Sustentatio* for the Secular Clergy.
303. QUINN, REV. HUGH G., J.C.L., The Particular Penal Precept.
304. GALLAGHER, REV. JOHN F., J.C.L., The Matrimonial Impediment of Public Propriety.
305. WELSH, REV. THOMAS J., J.C.L., The Use of the Portable Altar.

www.ingramcontent.com/pod-product-compliance
Lightning Source LLC
LaVergne TN
LVHW050207080826
844660LV00012B/373

9780813224695